Published by

Electric Adventures 1991

Rokeby Tasmania 7019, Australia

Republished by

Electric Adventures 2016

Bellerive Tasmania 7018, Australia

Table of Contents

Introduction

This book is a compilation of information to assist the owners of Spectravideo 318/328 machines and their MSX cousins. The Spectravideo and MSX machines are wonderful computers to learn to program. On them with very little effort you can make a TV screen come alive with fantastic colour pictures and make sound burst forth from the TV speakers. Also you can play great games, learn how to program and let the computer teach you other subjects like maths and spelling. Also once disk drives and perhaps a printer are added, they can be used for more serious purposes like storing information and word processing.

But there is only one person who can make your computer come alive. YOU! So read on and hopefully this book will assist you in your exploration of your computer.

Important Facts

Spectravideo Basic and MSX Basic are an extended version of Microsoft Basic Version 5, which includes support of graphics, music and various peripherals attached to the Spectravideo 318/328 and MSX compatible Personal Computers. Generally, the Basic is designed to follow GW-Basic which is standard in 16-bit computers (i.e. I.B.M.-PC). But a major effort has been made to make the whole system flexible and expandable.

Also the Basic is featured with up to 14 digits of accuracy using double precision BCD arithmetic function. This means arithmetic operations no longer generate strange rounding errors. Every transcendental function is also calculated with this accuracy. 16 signed integer operation is also available for very fast execution.

Note: From now on in the manual I will be referring to Spectravideo Basic as SVI Basic.

Operational Modes

When Basic is initialised it displays the prompt 'Ok'. This indicates Basic is at command level; that is, it is ready to accept commands. At this point, Basic may be used in either of two modes:

Direct Mode:

Basic statements and commands are not preceded by line numbers. They are executed as they are entered. Results of arithmetic and logic operations may be displayed immediately and stored for later use, but the instructions themselves are lost after execution. Direct mode is useful for debugging and for using Basic as a calculator for quick computations that do not require a complete program.

Indirect Mode:

This is used for entering programs. Program lines are preceded by line numbers and are stored in memory. The program stored in memory is executed by entering the **RUN** command.

The Format of Lines

Basic program lines have the following format (square brackets indicate optional input):

```
nnnnn BASIC statement: BASIC statement… [Enter]
```

More than one Basic statement may be placed on a line, but each must be separated from the last by a colon (:).

A Basic program line always begins with a line number and ends when you press the [Enter] key. A line may contain a maximum of 255 characters.

Line Numbering

Every Basic program begins with a line number. Line numbers indicate the order I which the program lines are stored in memory. Line numbers are also used as references in branching and editing. Line numbers must be in the range 0 to 65525 and only integer type numbers can be used.

A period (.) may be used in **LIST**, **AUTO** and **DELETE** commands to refer to the current line.

Legal Characters

The Basic character set consists of alphabetic characters, numeric characters, special characters and graphic characters.

The alphabetic characters in Basic are the upper case and lower case letters of the alphabet.

The Basic numeric characters are the digits 0 to 9.

In addition: the following special characters are recognised by Basic:

Character	Action
	Blank
=	Equals sign
+	Plus sign
-	Minus sign
*	Asterisk or Multiplication symbol
/	Slash or Division symbol
^	Up arrow or Exponentiation symbol
(	Left parenthesis
)	Right parenthesis
%	Percentage
#	Number sign
$	Dollar sign
!	Exclamation point
,	Comma
.	Period or Decimal Point
'	Single quotation mark or apostrophe
<	Less than
>	Greater than
\	Back slash or integer division symbol
@	At sign
_	Underscore
<rubout>	Deletes last character typed. (Large arrow key pointing left)
<escape>	Escape (ESC key)
<tab>	Moves print position to next tab stop. Tab stops are set every 5 columns. (Large arrow key pointing right)
<carriage return>	Terminates input of a line (Large key marked ENTER).

Using Constants

Constants are the values Basic uses during execution. There are two types of constants: String and Numeric.

String Constants: Are a sequence of up to 255 alphanumeric characters enclosed in double quotation marks.

Examples:

```
"Fred"
"$1,250,000.00"
"Spectravideo Basic is the best."
```

Numeric Constants: Are positive or negative numbers. Basic numeric constants cannot contain commas. There are six types of numeric constants:

1. Integer Constants: Whole numbers between -32768 and 32767. Integer constants do not contain decimal points.
2. Fixed Point Constants: Positive or negative real numbers i.e. numbers that contain decimal points.
3. Floating Point Constants: Positive or negative numbers represented in exponential form (similar to scientific notation). A floating-point constant consists of an optionally signed integer or fixed-point number (the Mantissa) followed by the letter E and an optionally signed integer (the Exponent). The allowable range for floating-point constants is 10 E-64 to 10 E+63.
   Examples:
   ```
   197.899E-7 = 0.0000197899
   6618E6 = 6618000000
   ```
   (Double precision floating-point constants are denoted by the letter D instead of E.)
4. Hex Constants: Hexadecimal numbers are denoted by the prefix &H.
   Examples:
   ```
   &H34
   &HFC
   ```

5. Octal Constants: Octal numbers are denoted by the prefix &O or &.

   Examples:

   ```
   &O172
   &.4321
   ```

6. Binary Constants: Binary numbers are denoted by the prefix &B.

   Examples:

   ```
   &B10110001
   &B11101100
   ```

Single and Double Precision Numeric Constants

Numeric constants may be either single precision or double precision numbers. Single precision numeric constants are stored with 6 digits of precision. Double precision numeric constants are stored with 14 digits of precision and printed with up to 14 digits of precision. Double precision is the default for constants in Basic.

A single precision constant is any numeric constant that has one of the following characteristics:

1. Exponential form using E.
2. A trailing exclamation point (!).

   Examples:

   ```
   -7.32E-09
   79.5!
   ```

A double precision constant is any numeric constant that has one of these characteristics:

1. Any digit or number without an exponential or type specifier.
2. Exponential form using D.
3. A trailing number sign (#).

   Examples:

   ```
   7182
   911615378
   -7.49302D-07
   2376.0#
   5768970.3578
   ```

Program Variables

Variables are names used to represent values used in a Basic program. The value of a variable may be assigned explicitly by the programmer, or it may be assigned as a result of calculations in the program. Before a variable is assigned a value, its value is assumed to be zero.

Variable Naming and Declaration

Basic variable names may be any length. Up to 2 characters are significant. Variable names can contain letters and numbers. However, the first character must be a letter. Special type declaration characters are also allowed (see below).

A variable name may not be a reserved word and may not contain embedded reserved words. Reserved words include all Basic commands (statements) function names and operator names. If a variable begins with FN, it is assumed to be a call to a user-defined function.

Variables may represent a numeric value or a string. String variable names are written with a dollar sign ($) as the last character. For example: A$ = "Merry Christmas". The dollar sign is a variable type declaration character; that is, it "declares" that the variable will represent a string.

Numeric variable names may be declared as integer, single precision or double precision values. The type declaration characters for these variable names are as follows:

%	Integer variable
!	Single Precision variable
#	Double Precision variable

The default type for a numeric variable name is double precision.

Examples of Basic variable names are:

X1#	Declares a double precision value.
MAP!	Declares a single precision value.
TEMP%	Declares an integer value.

P$	Declares a string value.
ZZY	Represents a double precision value.

There is a second method in which variable types may be declared. The Basic statements DEFINT, DEFSTR, DEFSMG and DEFDBL, may be included in a program to declare the types for certain variable names. Refer to the description for these statements.

The Array Variable

An array is a group or table of values referenced by the same variable name. Each element in an array is referenced by an array variable that is subscripted with an integer or an integer expression. An array variable name has as many subscripts as there are dimensions in the array. For example **B(17)** would reference a value in a one dimensional array, **Z(12,5,1)** would reference a value in a three dimensional array. The maximum number of elements is determined by memory size.

Space Requirements

The following table lists only the number of bytes occupied by the values represented by the variable names.

Variables

Type	Bytes
Integer	2
Single Precision	4
Double Precision	8

Arrays

Type	Bytes
Integer	2 per element
Single Precision	4 per element
Double Precision	8 per element

Strings

Three bytes overhead plus the present contents of the string.

Type Conversion

When necessary, Basic will convert a numeric constant from one type to another. The following rules and examples should be kept in mind.

1. If a numeric constant of one type is set equal to a numeric variable of a different type, the number will be stored as the type declared in the variable name. (If a string variable is set equal to a numeric value or vice a versa a **Type mismatch** error occurs.)

   Example:

   ```
   20 A% = 143.037
   30 PRINT A%
   RUN
    143
   Ok
   ```

2. During expression evaluation, all of the operands in an arithmetic or relational operation are converted to the same degree of precision i.e. that of the most precise operand. Also, the result of an arithmetic operation is returned to this degree of precision.

   Examples:

   The arithmetic was performed in double precision and the result was returned in D as a double precision value.

   ```
   10 D = 6/7!
   20 PRINT D
   RUN
    .85714285714286
   Ok
   ```

   The arithmetic was performed in double precision and the result was returned to D! (single precision variable), rounded, and printed as a single precision value.

   ```
   10 D! = 6/7
   20 PRINT D!
   RUN
    .857143
   Ok
   ```

3. Logical operators convert their operands to integers and return an integer result. Operands must be in the range -32768 to 32767 or an overflow error occurs.
4. When a floating point is converted to an integer, the fractional portion is truncated.

   Example:

   ```
   10 C% = 79.69
   20 PRINT C%
   RUN
    79
   Ok
   ```

5. If a double precision variable is assigned a single precision value, only the first 6 digits of the converted number will be valid. This is because only 6 digits of accuracy were supplied with the single precision value.

   Example:

   ```
   10 A! = SQR(2)
   20 B = A!
   30 PRINT A!,B
   RUN
    1.41421      1.41421
   Ok
   ```

Operators

An expression may be a string or numeric constant, a variable or a combination of constants and variables with operators which produce a single value.

Operators perform mathematical or logical operations on values. The Basic operators may be divided into 4 categories:

1. Arithmetic
2. Relational
3. Logical
4. Functional

Each category is described in the following sections.

Arithmetic Operators

The arithmetic operators in order of precedence are:

Operator	Operation	Sample Expression
^	Exponentiation	F^M
-	Negation	-F
* /	Multiplication, Floating point Division	F*M F/M
+ -	Addition, Subtraction	F+M F-M

To change the order in which the operations are performed, use parentheses. Operations within parentheses are performed first. Inside parentheses, the usual order of operations is maintained.

Integer Division and Modulus Arithmetic

Two additional operators are available in Basic; Integer division is denoted by the backslash symbol (\). The operands are truncated to integers (must be in the range -32768 to 32767) before the division is performed, and the quotient is truncated to an integer.

Example:

```
10\4  = 2
```

```
25.68\6.99 = 4
```

Integer division follows multiplication and floating point division in order of precedence. Modulus arithmetic is denoted by the operator MOD. Modules arithmetic yields the integer value that is the remainder of an integer division.

Example:

```
10.4 MOD 4 = 2 (10/4 = 2 with a remainder of 2)
25.68 MOD 6.99 = 1 (25/6 = 4 with a remainder of 1)
```

Modulus arithmetic follows integer division in order of precedence.

Overflow or Division by Zero

If during the evaluation of an expression **division by zero** is encountered the division by zero error message is displayed and execution terminates. If overflow occurs the overflow message is displayed and execution terminates.

Relational Operators

Relational operators are used to compare two values. The result of the comparison is either TRUE (-1) or FALSE (0). This result may then be used to make a decision regarding program flow. (See description for **IF** statements)

The relational operators are:

Operator	Relation Test	Example
=	Equality	F=M
<>	Inequality	F<>M
<	Less than	F<M
>	Greater than	F>M
<=	Less than or equal to	F<=M
>=	Greater than or equal to	F>=M

(The EQUAL sign is also used to assign a value to a variable.) When arithmetic and relational operators are combined in one expression, the arithmetic is always performed first. For example, the expression

```
F + M < (P - I)/L
```

Is true if the value of F plus M is less than the value of P minus I divided by L.

More examples:

```
IF COS(M)<0 GOTO 3000
IF P MOD F <> 0 THEN L = L + 3
```

Logical Operators

Logical operators perform tests on multiple relations, bit manipulation or Boolean operations. The logical operator returns a bit wise result, which is either TRUE (Not zero) or FALSE (zero). In an expression, logical operations are performed after arithmetic and relational operations. The outcome of a logical operation is determined as shown. The operators are listed in order of precedence.

Table 1 - Basic Relational Operators Truth Table

NOT	**X**	**NOT X**	
	1	0	
	0	1	
AND	**X**	**Y**	**X AND Y**
	1	1	1
	1	0	0
	0	1	0
	0	0	0
OR	**X**	**Y**	**X OR Y**
	1	1	1
	1	0	1
	0	1	1
	0	0	0
XOR	**X**	**Y**	**X XOR Y**
	1	1	0
	1	0	1
	0	1	1
	0	0	0
EQV	**X**	**Y**	**X EQV Y**
	1	1	1
	1	0	0
	0	1	0
	0	0	1
IMP	**X**	**Y**	**X IMP Y**
	1	1	1
	1	0	0
	0	1	1
	0	0	1

Just as the relational operators can be used to make decisions regarding program flow, logical operators can connect two or more relations and return a true or false value to be used in a decision.

Example:

```
IF M < 50 AND Z > 12 GOTO 1070
IF P > 11 OR PI < -5 GOTO 29
IF NOT M GOTO 1100
```

Logical operators work by converting their operands to 16 bit, signed, two's complement integers in the range -32768 to 32767. (If the operands are not in the range, an error results.) If both operands are supplied as 0 or -1, logical operators return 0 or -1. The given operation is performed on these integers in bit wise fashion i.e. each bit of the result is determined by the corresponding bits in the two operands.

Thus, it is possible to use logical operators to test bytes for a particular bit pattern. For instance, the AND operator may be used to MASK all bar one of the bits of a status byte at a machine I/O port. The OR operator may be used to merge two bytes to create a particular binary value. The following examples will help demonstrate how the logical operators work.

63 AND 16 = 16	63 = binary 111111 and 16 = binary 10000, so 63 AND 16 = 16
15 AND 14 = 14	15 = binary 1111 and 14 = binary 1110, so 15 AND 14 = 14
-1 AND 8 = 8	-1 = binary 1111111111111111 and 5 = binary 1000, so -1 AND 8 = 8
4 OR 2 = 6	4 = binary 100 and 2 = binary 10, so 4 OR 2 = 6
10 OR 10 = 10	10 = binary 1010, so 1010 OR 1010 = 1010
-1 OR -2 = -1	-1 = binary 1111111111111111 and -2 = binary 111111111111110, so -1 OR -2 = -1. The bit complement of sixteen zeros is sixteen ones, which is the two's complement representation.
NOT X = -(X + 1)	The twos complement of any integer is the bit complement plus one.

Functional Operators

A function is used in an expression to call a predetermined operation that is to be performed on an operand. Basic has intrinsic functions that reside in the system, such as **COS** (Cosine) or **TAN** (Tangent).

Basic also allows user defined functions that are written by the programmer. See descriptions for **DEF FN**.

String Operators

Strings may be concatenated by using "+".

Example:

```
10 M$="FRED": B$=" SMITH"
30 PRINT M$+B$
40 PRINT "Mr. ";M$+B$
RUN
 FRED SMITH
 Mr. FRED SMITH
Ok
```

Strings may be compared using the same relational operators that are used with numbers:

```
= <> <= >=
```

String comparisons are made by taking one character at a time from each string and comparing the ASCII codes. If all the ASCII codes are the same, the string is equal. If the ASCII code differ, the lower code number precedes the higher. If during string comparisons the end of one string is reached, the shorter string is said to be smaller. Leading and trailing blanks are significant.

Examples

```
"AA" < "AB"
"FRED" = "FRED"
"M&" > "M#"
"PD " > "PD"
"litre" > "LITRE"
```

```
"SMYTH" < "SMYTHE"
B$ < "3/10/84" where B$ = "2/10/84"
```

Thus, string comparisons can be used to test string values or to alphabetise strings. All string constants used in comparison expressions must be enclosed in quotation marks ("").

Editing of Programs

The full screen editor equipped with Basic allows the user to enter program lines as usual, then edit an entire screen before recording the changes. This time saving capability is made possible by the special keys for cursor movement, character insertion, character deletion and screen erasure. Specific functions and key assignments are discussed in the following sections.

With the full screen editor a user can move quickly around the screen, making corrections where necessary. The changes are entered by placing the cursor at the first line changed and pressing [Enter] at the beginning of each line. A program line is not actually changed until [Enter] is pressed from somewhere in the line.

Writing of Programs

Within Basic, the editor is in control any time after an **Ok** prompt and before a **RUN** command is issued. Any line of text that is entered is processed by the editor. Any line of text that begins with a number is considered a program statement.

Program statements are processed by the editor in one of the following ways:

1. A new line is added to the program. This occurs if the line number is value (0 through 65535) and at least one non-blank character follows the line number.

2. An existing line is modified. This occurs if the line number matches that of an existing line in the program. The existing line is replaced with the text of the new line.
3. An existing line is deleted. This occurs if the line number matches that of an existing line, and the new line contains only the line number.
4. An error is produced. If an attempt is made to delete a non-existing line, an **undefined line error** is displayed. If program memory is exhausted, and a line is added to the program, an **out of memory** error message is displayed and the line is not added.

More than one statement may be placed on a line. If this is done, the statements must be separated by a colon ":". The colon does not have to be surrounded by spaces.

The maximum number of characters that can be used in one program line, including the line number, is 255.

Editing Techniques

Use the **LIST** statement to display an entire program or range of lines on the screen so that they can be edited. Text can be modified by moving the cursor to the place where the change is needed and performing one of the following actions:

1. Typing over existing characters.
2. Deleting characters to the right of the cursor.
3. Deleting characters to the left of the cursor.
4. Inserting characters.
5. Appending characters to the end of the logical line.

These actions are performed by special keys assigned to the various full screen editor functions (see next section).

Changes to a line are record when the [Enter] key is pressed while the cursor is somewhere on the line. The [Enter] key enters all changes for that logical line, no matter how many physical lines are included and no matter where the cursor is located on the line.

The Full Screen Editor

The following table lists the hexadecimal codes for the Basic control characters and summarises their functions. The control key sequence normally assigned to each function is also listed. These conform as closely as possible to ASCII standard conversions.

Hex Code	Control Key	Special Key	Function
01	A		Ignored
02 *	B		Move cursor to start of previous word.
03 *	C		Break when Spectravideo Basic is waiting for input
04 *	D		Ignored
05 *	E		Truncate line (Clear text to end of logical line)
06 *	F		Move cursor to start of next word
07 *	G		Ignored
08 *	H	Back Space	Back space, deleting characters passed over
09 *	I	Tab	Tab (moves to next tab stop)
0A *	J		Line feed
0B *	K	Home	Move cursor to home position
0C *	L	CLS	Clear screen
0D *	M	ENTER	Carriage return (Enter current logical line)
0E *	N		Append to end of line
0F *	O		Ignored
10 *	P		Ignored
11 *	Q		Ignored
12 *	R	INS	Toggle insert/type over mode
13 *	S		Ignored
14 *	T		Ignored
15 *	U		Clear logical line
16 *	V		Ignored
17 *	W		Ignored
18 *	X		Select Ignored
19 *	Y		Ignored
1A *	Z		Ignored

1B *	[	ESC	Ignored
1C *	\	Right Arrow	Cursor right
1D *	]	Left Arrow	Cursor left
1E *	^	Up Arrow	Cursor up
1F *	_	Down Arrow	Cursor down
7F	DEL	DEL	Delete character at cursor

Control Functions. The ASCII control key is entered by pressing the key while holding down the control key (CTRL).

Note: Those keys marked with an asterisk (*) cancel insert mode when the editor is in insert mode.

Previous Word

The cursor is moved left to the previous word. The previous word is defined as the next character to the left of the cursor in the sets A-Z, a-z or 0-9.

Break

Returns to Spectravideo Basic direct mode, without saving changes that were made to the line currently being edited.

Truncate

The cursor is moved to the end of the logical line. The characters it passed over are deleted. Characters typed from the new cursor position are appended to the line.

Next Word

The cursor is moved right to the next word. The next word is defined as the next character to the right of the cursor in the sets A-Z, a-z or 0-9.

Backspace

Deletes the character to the left of the cursor. All characters to the right of the cursor are moved left one position.

Subsequent characters and lines within the current logical line are moved up (wrapped).

Tab

Tab moves the cursor to the next tab stop overwriting blanks Tab stops occur every 8 characters.

Cursor Home

Moves the cursor to the upper left corner of the screen. The screen is not blanked.

Clear Screen

Moves the cursor to the upper left corner of the screen and clears the entire screen, regardless of where the cursor is positioned when the key is pressed.

Enter

Sends a carriage return and ends the logical line thus sending it to Spectravideo Basic.

Append

Moves the cursor to the end of the line, without deleting the characters passed over. All characters typed from the new position until the [Enter] key is pressed are appended to the logical line.

Insert

Toggle switch for insert mode. When insert mode is on, the size of the cursor is reduced and characters are inserted at the current cursor location. Characters to the right of the cursor move right as new ones are inserted. Line wrap is observed. When insert mode is off, the size of the cursor returns to its normal size and typed characters will replace existing characters on the line.

Clear Logical Line

When this key is entered anywhere in the line, the entire logical line is erased.

Cursor Right

Moves the cursor one position to the right. Line wrap is observed.

Cursor Left

Moves the cursor one position to the left. Line wrap is observed.

Cursor Up

Moves the cursor up one physical line (at the current position).

Cursor Down

Moves the cursor down one physical line (at the current position).

Logical Line Definition with Input

Normally, a logical line consists of all the characters on each of the physical lines that make up the logical line. During execution of an **INPUT** or **LINE INPUT** statement, however, this definition is modified slightly to allow for forms input. When either of these statements is executed, the logical line is restricted to characters actually typed or passed over by the cursor. Insert mode and the delete function only move characters which are within that logical line and delete will decrement the size of the line.

Insert mode increments the logical line except when the characters moved will write over non-blank characters that are on the same physical line but not part of the logical line. In this case, the non-blank characters not part of the logical line are preserved and the characters at the end of the logical line are thrown out. This preserves labels that exist prior to the input statement. If an incorrect character is entered as a line is being typed, it can be deleted with the [Backspace] key or with control 'H'. Backspacing over a character erases it. Once a character(s) has been deleted, simply continue typing the line as desired.

To delete a line that is in the process of being typed, type Control-U.

To correct program lines for a program that is currently in memory, simply retype the line using the same line number. Basic automatically replaces the old line with the new line.

To delete the entire program currently residing in memory, enter the **NEW** command. **NEW** is usually used to clear memory prior to enter a new program.

CRT Terminal Emulation

The display for the Spectravideo Personal Computer emulates a terminal known as the DEV VT-52, is both the 40 column and 80 column modes. The following is a list of ESCAPE codes used by the terminal. Escape is decimal 26 and Hexadecimal 1B.

Sequence	Description
ESC E	Clears screen
ESC K	Erase to end of line
ESC J	Erase to end of page
ESC I	Clear line
ESC L	Insert line
ESC M	Delete line
ESC Y	Locate cursor, Y and X address follow with an offset of 32 (20H)
ESC A	Cursor up
ESC B	Cursor down
ESC C	Cursor right
ESC D	Cursor left
ESC H	Cursor home
ESC p	Start reverse video (SVI Basic Only)
ESC q	End reverse video (SVI Basic Only)
ESC x S	Turn Cursor off
ESC y S	Turn Cursor on

Example:

```
10 REM TURN ON INVERSE VIDEO
20 ESC=27
30 PRINT CHR$(ESC)+"p";"Hello"
40 REM TURN OFF INVERSE VIDEO
50 PRINT CHR$(ESC)+"q"
```

Function Keys

Basic supports special keys as follows.

Basic has 10 predefined function keys. The current contents of these keys are displayed on the last line of the screen and can be redefined by the **KEY** statement. The initial values for each key are:

Key Number	Definition
F1	color
F2	auto [cr]
F3	goto
F4	list
F5	run [cr]
F6	color 15,4,5 [cr]
F7	cload"
F8	cont [cr]
F9	list. [cr]
F10	[cls] run [cr]

Function keys are also used as event trap keys. See **ON KEY GOSUB** and **KEY ON/OFF/STOP** statements for details.

The [Stop] Key

When Basic is in command mode, the [Stop] key has no effect to the operation, Basic just ignores it.

When Basic is executing a program, pressing the [Stop] key causes suspension of the program execution and Basic then waits for another [Stop] key input to resume execution. If the [Stop] key and the control [CTRL] key are pressed simultaneously, Basic terminates the execution and returns to the command mode with the following message.

```
Break in nnnnn
```

where nnnnn is the program line number where the execution stopped.

Programming Techniques

Text on Graphic Screens

Using text on the graphic screens is different for SV and MSX. To use text on the SV screen 1 and 2, it is only necessary to position the invisible graphics cursor, using **LOCATE**, to the screen position where the text is to be displayed and then using the **PRINT** command. For example:

```
100 SCREEN 1
110 LOCATE 128.96
120 PRINT "ABC"
130 GOTO 130
```

For MSX the procedure is a little more complex. First a graphics file buffer must be opened and all text written to it. The **LOCATE** command does not work in graphics mode and must be replaced by **PRESET** (or any command that positions the graphics cursor). For example:

```
100 SCREEN 2
110 OPEN "GRP:" AS #1
120 PRESET (128,96)
130 PRINT #1,"ABC"
140 GOTO 140
```

Further complication arises when we want to accept text input from the keyboard while the program is in graphics mode. In text mode, **INPUT** could be used to accept the text. This command will destroy a graphics screen because it forces the computer back to text mode.

The alternative is to use **INKEY$** or **INPUT$(n)** for input. This is fine if you only require a one character response such as **Y** or **N** or a single digit. To accept a string of characters, such as a name, it is necessary to use a string input routine built around the **INKEY$** or **INPUT$(n)** commands. For example:

MSX Version

```
10 SCREEN 2,2
20 OPEN "GRP:" AS #1
30 LINE(10,10)-(245,181),5,BF
40 PRESET(10,100) : PRINT #1,"NAME"
50 X=72
60 I$=INKEY$: IF I$="" THEN 60
70 PRESET(X,100) : X=X+8
80 IF I$>CHR$(13) THEN PRINT #1,I$: GOTO 60
```

- Line 20 opens the file buffer
- Line 30 puts graphics on the screen
- Line 40 prints the prompt
- Line 60 waits for I$ to have a value
- Line 70 locates the graphics cursor
- Line 80 checks if the key is [Enter] – if not, display the character and go back and wait for the next one

SVI Version

```
10 SCREEN 1,2
20 LINE(10,10)-(245,181),5,BF
30 LOCATE 10,100: PRINT "NAME"
40 X=72
50 I$=INKEY$: IF I$="" THEN 50
60 LOCATE X,100: X=X+8
70 IF I$>CHR$(13) THEN PRINT I$: GOTO 50
```

- Line 20 puts graphics on the screen
- Line 30 prints the prompt
- Line 50 waits for I$ to have a value
- Line 60 locates the graphics cursor
- Line 70 checks if the key is [Enter], if not, display the character and go back for the next

Converting MSX Basic Programs to SVI Basic

Spectravideo Basic and MSX Basic are very similar, and not many changes need to be made to convert programs between the two Basics. This section outlines the things to change between the two Basics. To start first make a careful study of the MSX listing. The first thing to look for are the **SCREEN** commands. The Spectravideo uses **SCREEN 0** for text, and **SCREEN 1** and **2** for graphics and sprites. MSX uses **SCREEN 0** for text (no problem there), **SCREEN 1** for text and sprites, **SCREEN 2** and **3** for graphics and sprites. If the program contains a **SCREEN 1** command, then it will be almost impossible to convert it because the Spectravideo does not use this screen mode.

Another thing to watch for are graphics characters which are entered from the keyboard. The Spectravideo uses a **LEFT GRAPH** and **RIGHT GRAPH** key to produce 52 block graphics from the alphabetical keys on the keyboard. The MSX, on the other hand uses a **GRAPH** key and **SHIFT+GRAPH** to produce 87 block graphics and a **CODE** key and **SHIFT+CODE** to produce a range of non-English letters and symbols. There are a few similarities between the block graphics used by the two machines.

Comparison chart of SVI and MSX Block Graphic Characters

SV Character	MSX Character	SV Character	MSX Character
160 (LEFT+A)	20 (GRAPH+F)	183 (LEFT+X)	17 (GRAPH+B)
161 (LEFT+B)	223 (SHIFT+GRAPH+I)	184 (LEFT+Y)	214 (SHIFT+GRAPH+H)
162 (LEFT+C)	27 (GRAPH+N)	185 (LEFT+Z)	26 (GRAPH+V)
163 (LEFT+D)	19 (GRAPH+H)	187 (RIGHT+B)	3 (SHIFT+GRAPH+,)
164 (LEFT+E)	25 (GRAPH+Y)	188 (RIGHT+C)	29 (GRAPH+/)
165 (LEFT+F)	222 (SHIFT+GRAPH+K)	189 (RIGHT+D)	28 (GRAPH+X)
166 (LEFT+G)	193 (SHIFT+GRAPH+D)	190 (RIGHT+E)	30 (GRAPH+\)
167 (LEFT+H)	221 (GRAPH+K)	191 (RIGHT+F)	9 (GRAPH+O)
173 (LEFT+N)	211 (SHIFT+GRAPH+N)	192 (RIGHT+6)	199 (GRAPH+D)
176 (LEFT+Q)	24 (GRAPH+R)	198 (RIGHT+M)	5 (GRAPH+,)
177 (LEFT+R)	12 (SHIFT+GRAPH+F)	199 (RIGHT+N)	4 (SHIFT+GRAPH+;)
178 (LEFT+S)	21 (GRAPH+G)	201 (RIGHT+P)	219 (GRAPH+O)
179 (LEFT+T)	220 (GRAPH+U)	207 (RIGHT+V)	6 (GRAPH+;)
181 (LEFT+V)	213 (SHIFT+GRAPH+V)	209 (RIGHT+X)	23 (GRAPH+-)
182 (LEFT+W)	18 (GRAPH+T)	211 (RIGHT+Z)	22 (SHIFT+GRAPH+\)

If the program does not contain a **SCREEN 1** command or any graphics characters from the keyboard, then it is probably quite safe to go ahead and type the listing in – provided you can be sure that it worked in the original MSX version.

If the program listing has been reproduced from a dot matrix printout, then there is every chance that it is an unadulterated listing of a program that runs. Be cautious of listings where there are no slashes through the zeroes in the line numbers. If they look like a capital letter **O** then you will have a great difficulty in some cases determining whether it is an **O** or a zero in the body of the listing. Even worse are listings which have been produced on a typewriter which uses a lower case letter l for the number 1.

Using Random Access Files

The following example makes use of the **OPEN, FIELD, LSET, PUT, GET, MKI$** and **CVI** commands. It requests input of eight names, addresses and phone numbers and saves these into the random access file called **FILE.** It then allows you to search each record by inputting the number of that record.

```
10 REM MAKE ROOM FOR STRINGS
20 CLEAR 1000
30 REM OPEN FILE
40 OPEN "1:FILE" AS #1 (SVI)
40 OPEN "FILE" AS #1 (MSX)
50 REM FIELD THE BUFFER
60 FIELD #1,8 AS A$, 30 AS A2$, 30 AS A3$, 30 AS A4$,
30 AS A5$
70 REM LOOP FOR RECORD COLLETION
80 FOR I=1 TO 8
90 CLS
100 PRINT "RECORD #";I
110 INPUT "NAME: ";NM$
120 INPUT "STREET: ";ST$
130 INPUT "SUBURB: ";SU$
140 INPUT "PHONE: ";PH$
150 REM PLACE IN BUFFER FIELDS
160 LSET A1$=MKI$(I)
170 LSET A2$=NM$
180 LSET A3$=ST$
190 LSET A4$=SU$
200 LSET A5$=PH$
210 REM PUT BUFFER TO DISK
220 PUT #1,I
230 NEXT I
240 REM SEARCH RECORDS BY NUMBER
250 CLS: PRINT "SEARCH …"
260 INPUT "RECORD NUMBER 1-8";R
270 REM LOAD INTO BUFFER FROM DISK
280 GET#1,R
290 RN=CVI(A1$)
300 PRINT "RECORD #";RN
310 PRINT "NAME: ";A2$
```

```
320 PRINT "STREET: ";A3$
330 PRINT "SUBURB: ";A4$
340 PRINT "PHONE: ";A5$
350 PRINT
360 INPUT "ANOTHER RECORD (Y/N)";I$
370 IF I$="Y" OR I$="y" THEN 250
380 REM FINISHED WITH FILE SO CLOSE BUFFER
390 CLOSE #1
```

Writing Games

To show how you can write your own games, we will work our way through a complete game. We will be looking at the separate sections that make up the game, describing them in more detail.

The game we will look at is called 'Eliminator' and is an arcade shoot-em-up. The idea of the game is to stop the aliens from capturing all the humans from Earth. Your ship is equipped with a high powered laser cannon and can take several direct hits. Your ship can only go in one horizontal direction, but can speed up and slow down. You have to shoot the aliens as they move down the screen towards the humans on the surface of the Earth at the bottom of the screen. If you let an alien reach Earth, it will capture a human and start moving to the top of the screen. You have to shoot the alien before it reaches the top of the screen or the human will be lost!

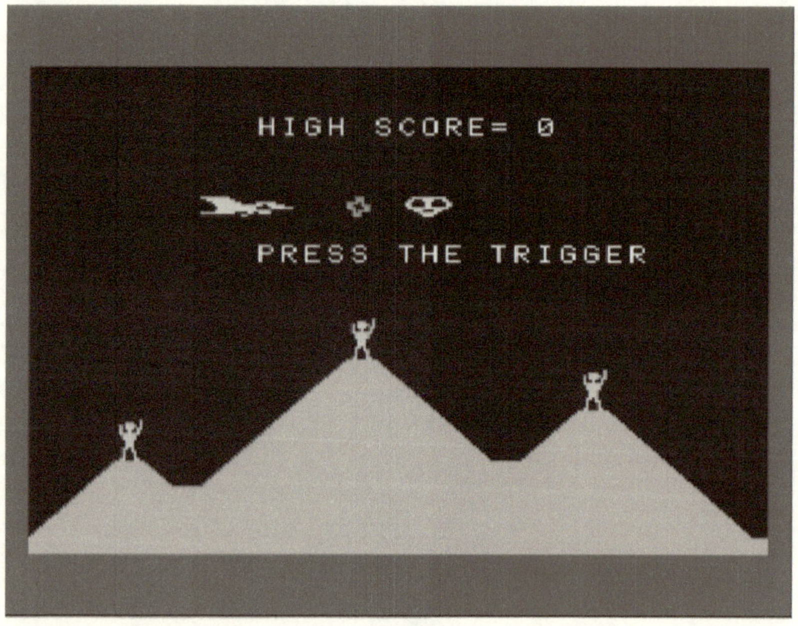

```
10 COLOR15,1:SCREEN2,2:A=RND(-TIME):DEFINTA-
Y:DEFSNGL,Z:ZH=1000:DIMPX(3),PY(3),T(3):OPEN"GRP:"AS#
1
20 DEFFNA(X)=INT(RND(1)*X)+1:A1$="C14S4BM0,185E30R10
F10R10E50R10F40R10E20R10F50"
30 FORA=1TO5:S$="":READA$:FORB=1TOLEN(A$)STEP2:S$=S$
+CHR$(VAL("&H"+MID$(A$,B,2))):NEXT:SPRITE$(A)=S$:NEXT
40 CLS:LINE(0,185)-(256,192),14,BF:DRAW A1$:PAINT
(10,184),14:PRESET(80,70):PRINT #1,"PRESS THE
TRIGGER"
50 PRESET(80,20):PRINT#1,"HIGH SCORE=";HI:PUT SPRITE
1,(60,50),11,1:PUT SPRITE 2,(76,50),11,2
60 PUT SPRITE 4,(110,50),9,5:PUT SPRITE 5,(112,98)
,7,4:PUT SPRITE 6,(32,138),7,4:PUT SPRITE
7,(192,118),7,4
70 PUT SPRITE 3,(130,50),3,3
80 IF NOT(STRIG(0)+STRIG(1)) THEN 80 ELSE
CLS:ZS=0:GOSUB 670
90 RESTORE 730:FOR A=1 TO 3:READ PX(A),PY(A):
T(A)=1:NEXT:H=0: C=10: B=0: A1=0: M=3 :CA=0: L=1:
A9=0: M1=1: B1=0: LH=0
100 LINE(0,185)-(256,192),14,BF:DRAW
A1$:PAINT(10,184),14:FOR A=1 TO 3:PUT SPRITE
3+A,(PX(A),PY(A)),7,4:NEXT:X=1:Y=96
110 IF A1=0 THEN AX=FNA(100)+100:AY=5:A1=1:GOTO 160
120 IF A1=2 THEN AY=AY-L:PUT SPRITE
3+M,(AX,AY+8),7,4:IF AY<-25 THEN M=M-1:A1=0:GOTO 190
ELSE 160
130 IF AX>PX(M) THEN AX=AX-5:GOTO 150
140 IF AX<PX(M) THEN AX=AX+5
150 AY=AY+5:IF AY>=PY(M) AND T(M)<>0 THEN A1=2:T(M)=0
160 PUT SPRITE 2,(AX,AY),3,3
170 SOUND 8,0:IF LH>0 THEN LH=LH-1:LINE(0,180)-
(200,190)
,14,BF:LINE(0,180)-(LH*4,190),9,BF:IF LH>40 THEN
H=H+1:C=C-1
180 IF LH>20 THEN SOUND 8,8:SOUND 0,200:SOUND 1,1
190 IF B=0 THEN MX=AX:MY=AY:B=15:GOTO 250
200 IF MX>X THEN MX=MX-3:GOTO 220
210 IF MX<X THEN MX=MX+3
```

```
220 IF MY>Y THEN MY=MY-3:GOTO 240
230 IF MY<Y THEN MY=MY+3
240 B=B-1:IF B=0 THEN PUT SPRITE 3,(1,209):GOTO 260
250 PUT SPRITE 3,(MX,MY),9,5:IF MX<X+32 AND MX>X-4
AND MY<MY+8 AND MY>Y-4 THEN PUT SPRITE
3,(1,209):B=0:H=H+1:C=C-1
260 GOSUB 500:IF M=0 OR H=3 OR M1=3 OR 3-M+M1=3 THEN
440
270 X=X+10:A=STICK(0)+STICK(1)
280 IF X>256 THEN X=X-256
290 IF A=1 THEN Y=Y-8:IF Y<5 THEN Y=5
300 IF A=3 THEN X=X+5
310 IF A=5 THEN Y=Y+10:IF Y>180 THEN Y=180
320 IF A=7 THEN X=X-5
330 PUT SPRITE 0,(X,Y),C,1:PUT SPRITE 1,(X+16,Y),C,2
340 IF NOT(STRIG(0)+STRIG(1)) OR Y>106 THEN 110
350 LH=LH+5:LINE(X+32,Y+6)-(256,Y+6)
360 SOUND 8,8:SOUND 9,8:SOUND 1,3:SOUND 0,255: SOUND
3,1:SOUND 2,255
370 IF AX>X+28 AND AY<Y+8 AND AY>Y-8 THEN PUT SPRITE
2,(1,209): L=L+.1: A8=1: ZS=ZS+10: IF A1=2 THEN PUT
SPRITE 3+M,(PX(M),PY(M)),7,4:ZS=ZS+40:T(M)=1
380 IF A8=1 THEN GOSUB 480:A1=0
390 A8=0
400 IF MX>X+28 AND MY<Y+8 AND MY>Y-8 THEN PUT SPRITE
3,(1,209):ZS=ZS+5:B=0
410 GOSUB 640:A2$=INKEY$
420 LINE(X+32,Y+6)-(256,Y+6),1
430 SOUND 8,0:SOUND 9,0:GOTO 110
440 SOUND 8,0:SOUND 9,0:SOUND 10,0:FOR A=1 TO
1000:NEXT:PRESET(100,80):PRINT #1,"GAME OVER"
450 PRESET(100,100):PRINT #1,"SCORE=";ZS
460 IF ZS>ZH THEN ZH=ZS:GOSUB 490
470 FOR A=1 TO 4000:NEXT:GOSUB 670:GOTO 40
480 PLAY "","","L10M2000A11N10":RETURN
490 PLAY :"L10O5A-A-G-O3G-":RETURN
500 IF A9=0 THEN X1=FNA(100)+100:Y1=5:A9=1:GOTO 550
510 IF A9=2 THEN Y1=Y1-L:PUT SPRITE
3+M1,(X1,Y1+8),7,4:IF Y1<25 THEN M1=M1+1:A9=0:GOTO
560 ELSE 500
520 IF X1>PX(M1) THEN X1=X1-5:GOTO 540
```

```
530 IF X1<PX(M1) THEN X1=X1+5
540 Y1=Y1+5:IF Y1>PY(M1) AND T(M1)<>0 THEN
A9=2:T(M1)=0
550 PUT SPRITE 7,(X1,Y1),3,3
560 IF B1=0 THEN X2=X1:Y2=Y1:B1=15:GOTO 620
570 IF X2>X THEN X2=X2-3:GOTO 590
580 IF X2<X THEN X2=X2+3
590 IF Y2>Y THEN Y2=Y2-3:GOTO 610
600 IF Y2<Y THEN Y2=Y2+3
610 B1=B1-1:IF B=0 THEN PUT SPRITE 8,(1,209):GOTO 630
620 PUT SPRITE 8,(X2,Y2),9,5:IF X2<X+32 AND X2>X-4
AND Y2<Y+8 AND Y2>Y-4 THEN PUT SPRITE
8,(1,209):B1=0:H=H+1:C=C-1
630 RETURN
640 IF X1>X+28 AND Y1<Y+8 AND Y1>Y-8 THEN PUT SPRITE
7,(1,209):L=L+.1:ZS=ZS+10:GOSUB 480:IF A9=2 THEN PUT
SPRITE 3+M1,(PX(M1),PY(M2)),7,4:ZS=ZS+40:T(M1)=1:A9=0
ELSE A9=0
650 IF X2>X+28 AND Y2<Y+8 AND Y2>Y-8 THEN PUT SPRITE
8,(1,209):SZ=SZ+5:B1=0
660 RETURN
670 FOR A=0 TO 31:VPOKE 6912+A*4,209:NEXT:RETURN
680 DATA
FF3F0F070307FF000000000000000000C0F0FCFFFFFFF003
690 DATA 00001FF9E0FFCF0000000000000000000000C0F8FF
700 DATA
3F63C1C17F1C07030000000000000000FCC68383FE38E0C0
710 DATA 0139BDBB92FE7C7C383838684C4444C6
720 DATA 1C1CF4C7E32F3838
730 DATA 112,98,32,138,192,118
```

Line by line break down of the program:

10 First we must set out background colour and select the screen mode we want to use (high resolution mode). To make sure any random numbers are different from the last time we ran the program we use A = RND(-TIME). The rest of the line sets most of the variables to integers (except the score and high score which may get larger

than 32767), declares some arrays we will use for the humans and opens a file to the graphics screen.

20 DEFFNA(X) sets a random number function that we can use to get a number between 0 and X. In A1$ we put a string of drawing commands that will draw the mountain landscape on the screen.

30 This line reads in the sprite shapes stored in the data at the end of the program. Each DATA line contains one complete sprite shape. Each pair of digits e.g. FF is a hexadecimal number that represents the pattern of the sprite. This takes a lot less space than writing the shapes in binary where FF would need 16 ones to represent. The only disadvantage of this method is that it is hard to see what the sprite shapes look like.

40 Now we clear the screen and draw our landscape with a filled block at the bottom of the screen and the drawing commands we stored in A1$ earlier. To tell the person using the game that they need to press the joystick trigger to start the game we print a message using PRINT #1. This sends the text to device one, which we set up earlier to be the graphics screen. Notice the PRESET command was used to set where the text was to appear.

50 Now the current high score is displayed along with the main ship which is made up of two sprites.

60-70 To make a more exciting title screen to the game, a few more sprites are displayed on the screen.

80 By adding the result of the two STRIG statements we quickly check both the keyboard trigger (the spacebar) and the trigger of joystick one. This if will just loop to the same line until either trigger is pressed. Once a

trigger has been pressed, we clear the screen, set the score to zero and jump to a subroutine that clears all the sprites from the screen.

90 This line restores the data pointer to the data statement that contains the position of the humans and reads the data into the arrays we declared earlier. The rest of the line sets up all the variables we will be using in the program.

100 This line redraws the mountain places the humans, and sets the coordinates of the main ship.

110 This is the first line of our main game loop. First we start by putting the first alien on the screen, if he is not already there. The alien is placed at a random position along the top of the screen. A1 is set to one so we know the alien has already been placed.

120 This line tests if A1=2, if this is the case then our alien has a human in tow and is moving up the screen. So the aliens Y coordinate (AY) is made smaller using our level variable L and the human in tow is placed just below the alien on the screen. If the top of the screen is reached then the number of humans left (M) is decreased and we skip the actual placing of the alien on the screen. Otherwise we jump to line 160.

130-140 These two lines examine where the next human in line to be taken is in relation to the alien and make the alien move left or right accordingly.

150 Here the Y coordinate of the alien is changed. If the alien is low enough and the human it was going for has not disappeared, the variable A1 is set to two so that we will know to start moving it back up the screen. The

variable T() is used to make sure that we know that this human is being captured by an alien already.

160 Here we place the alien on the screen.

170 First we stop any sounds from sound channel zero. Then if the laser heat counter (LH) is larger than zero i.e. the laser has been fired, a red bar is drawn at the bottom of the screen to show how hot the laser is.

180 If the laser is getting too hot a warning tone is started, using sound channel zero.

190 If the first alien bullet is not already on the screen, it is placed at the current position of the alien. The variable B is set to 15. This is the number of times the bullet will move before it disappears.

200-230 These lines change the bullets coordinates so that they follow the main ship.

240 Here the bullet timer is decremented and the bullet sprite removed from the screen if B has reached zero.

250 Here the bullet is placed on the screen. The bullet's coordinates are compared with those of the main ship. If the bullet has hit the main ship the hit counter is increased and the bullet removed from the screen.

260 Here we jump to a subroutine that places the second alien and bullet. A more correct way of programming this section would have been to use arrays (like what was done for the humans) and using a loop. The next line tests to see if the main ship has been hit too many times or if all the humans have been taken away.

270 Now we move the main ship to the right and read the joystick (including the keyboard joystick/cursor keys).

280	If the ship has moved off the right hand side of the screen the ship is moved back to the left hand side.
290-320	These lines move the ship according to the direction the joystick was moved in.
330	Here we put the two sprites that make up the main ship.
340	Now we test if the joystick trigger has been pressed (including the spacebar). If it has not been pressed we jump back to the start of the main loop.
350	The laser heat variable (LH) is increased and we draw the laser on the screen using the line command.
360	Now we use the SOUND command to make a zap sound for the laser.
370	Now we test if the laser hit the alien. If it did the score is increased and if the alien was carrying a human, the human is put back at the bottom of the screen. An extra point bonus is added to the score for saving the human.
380	This line jumps to a subroutine if we hit the alien, to make a sound for the alien dying.
390	Resetting our alien dying flag.
400	Now we test if the laser hit the alien's bullet. If so the score is increased and the bullet removed from the screen.
410	Now we jump to a subroutine to repeat the collision tests for the second alien and bullet. Once again we could have benefited from a loop and array variables here.
420	Now we draw a line to erase our laser from the screen.

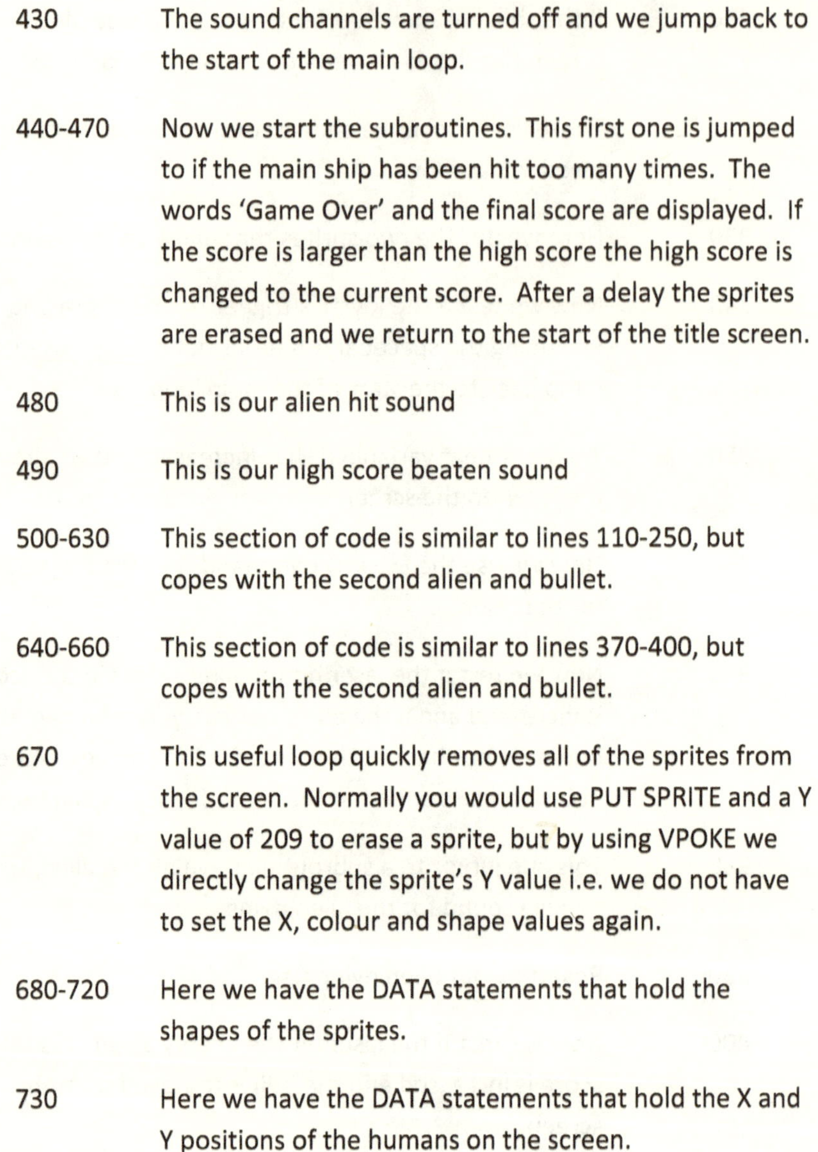

430	The sound channels are turned off and we jump back to the start of the main loop.
440-470	Now we start the subroutines. This first one is jumped to if the main ship has been hit too many times. The words 'Game Over' and the final score are displayed. If the score is larger than the high score the high score is changed to the current score. After a delay the sprites are erased and we return to the start of the title screen.
480	This is our alien hit sound
490	This is our high score beaten sound
500-630	This section of code is similar to lines 110-250, but copes with the second alien and bullet.
640-660	This section of code is similar to lines 370-400, but copes with the second alien and bullet.
670	This useful loop quickly removes all of the sprites from the screen. Normally you would use PUT SPRITE and a Y value of 209 to erase a sprite, but by using VPOKE we directly change the sprite's Y value i.e. we do not have to set the X, colour and shape values again.
680-720	Here we have the DATA statements that hold the shapes of the sprites.
730	Here we have the DATA statements that hold the X and Y positions of the humans on the screen.

Now a more recent version of this listing could have been included in the book, but then there would have been less things for you to change. The most effective way of learning about your machine is to change this program around to suit your own desires. This way you can slowly discover what effect some putting in some different values on each of the commands.

As a start you could try and improve the program so that the aliens and bullets are handled in the one section of code, using a loop and some array variables. Then you could try increasing the loop so that more aliens and bullets appear. One cautionary note though, try not to add too many moving objects or the game will become too slow to play.

It's on the Disk (or tape)!

If you are feeling a bit daunted by the amount of typing needed to try out the above programs, then you can load the listings into your computer using the optional disk (or tape) for this book. It also contains a bonus program called 'Sprite Definer'. This program allows you to design your own sprite shapes on screen. The codes produced, can be written down and entered into your own programs.

Beyond Basic – Part 1

Written By: Tony Cruise

First Published: MSX and Spectravideo Computer Forum Vol. 2 No. 10

Introduction

What I aim to do in this series of articles is to provide an insight into machine code programming on your computer. The articles will take for granted that you know how to program in BASIC, but will not require knowledge of machine code. Full machine code listings will be included for the person who wants to know more, but they will not be necessary for understanding the article.

The series of programs will eventually add extra commands that you can use in your BASIC programs.

The sections will include:-

- Making use of all 64k of your computer's memory
- Printer dump routines
- Screen save and load to memory and/or tape and disk
- Automatic sprite movement with velocities
- Sprite collision detection
- Screen scrolling routines

Part 1 – Using More Memory

A lot of the original MSX game titles that used more than 32K of RAM were very machine dependant. A classic example is "Finders Keepers" which only works on the Sony HIT-BIT. The author took it for granted that all of the MSX machines would have their RAM in the same area. To explain this further look at the diagram below:

0000H	Slot 0	Slot 1	Slot 2	Slot 3	
	ROM		SONY RAM		Page 0
4000H					
	ROM		SONY RAM		Page 1
8000H					
	ROM		SONY RAM		Page 2
C000H					
	ROM		SONY RAM		Page 3
FFFFH					

Any of the boxes in the picture can hold 16K of RAM or ROM (Up to 64K can be placed in each box, but that is beyond the scope of this article). Only one of the four slots can be activated for each page of memory. Thus when you turn on the computer the BASIC ROM is activated, so only the top 32K of RAM can be accessed. This is why you only get 28K of RAM free for your BASIC programs (The other 4K of RAM is used by BASIC as a storage space for system variables e.g. cursor position).

Machine Code Program

	1 ORIGIN	ORG 08400H	
	2 ;		
	3 ; PROGRAM TO FIND EXTRA RAM IN MSX COMPUTERS		
	4 ;		
F3	5 START	DI	; Disables all interrupts
DBA8	6	IN A,(0A8H)	; Get page settings
4F	7	LD C,A	; Store in C
0603	8	LD B,3	; Loop counter
210000	9	LD HL,0	; Memory location to test
C5	10 LP1	PUSH BC	; Save BC
79	11	LD A,C	;
B0	12	OR B	;
CB20	13	SLA B	;
CB20	14	SLA B	;
B0	15	OR B	; Calculate slot
D3AB	16	OUT (0A8H),A	; Send bank information
C1	17	POP BC	; Restore BC
3E01	18	LD A,1	;
77	19	LD (HL),A	;
7E	20	LD A,(HL)	;
3D	21	DEC A	;
2802	22	JR Z,EXIT	; Is it RAM
10EC	23	DJNZ LP1	; Do loop again
78	24 EXIT	LD A,B	;
B1	25	OR C	;
CB20	26	SLA B	;
CB20	27	SLA B	;
B0	28	OR B	; Calculate slot
32E7FF	29	LD (0FFE7H),A	; Store in 0FFE7H
79	30	LD A,C	; Set pages to normal
D3AB	31	OUT (0A8H),A	;
FB	32	EI	; Enable interrupts
C(	33	RET	; Return to BASIC

Basic Loader

```
10 CLS:CLEAR 200,&HCFFF:DEFINTA-Z:A=&HD000
20 READ A$:IF A$ <> "@" THEN POKE A,
VAL("&H"+A$):A=A+1:GOTO 20
30 PRINT"  INSERT TAPE/DISK TO SAVE PROGRAM"
40 PRINT"          AND PRESS ANY KEY"
50 A$=INPUT$(1):PRINT:PRINT "  SAVING ...."
```

```
60 BSAVE"CAS:RAMSEL",&HD000,A-1:REM Remove CAS:
if using disk
100 DATA F3,DB,A8,4F,06,03,21,00,00,C5
110 DATA 79,B0,CB,20,CB,20,B0,D3,A8,C1
120 DATA 3E,01,77,7E,3D,28,02,10,EC,78
130 DATA B1,CB,20,CB,20,B0,32,E7,FF,79
140 DATA D3,A8,FB,C9
150 DATA @
```

Beyond Basic – Part 2

Written By: Tony Cruise

First Published: MSX and Spectravideo Computer Forum Vol. 2 No. 11

Introduction

In this section I will explain how you attach extra commands to ROM routines.

In MSX computers there are many Hook Jumps provided so that machine code programmers can attach their own routines to most of the basic ROM routines. Each Hook consists of five memory locations in RAM. When the computer is first switched on or reset, each of the locations contains the value 201. This is the decimal value for a RETURN statement in machine code. Each of the Hooks are jumped to at the start of each of the corresponding ROM routines, so you can insert or eliminate entirely each routine.

To use a Hook, all you have to do is insert your own commands into the five memory locations. This is usually a JUMP instruction to your machine code routine.

Here is an example program that uses the Hook HTIMI. This Hook is jumped to every 1/50th of a second.

Machine Code Program

D000		1 ORIGIN	ORG 0D000H	
		2 ;		
		3 ; PROGRAM TO UPDATE AND DISPLAY A CLOCK		
		4 ; ON SCREEN 0		
		5 ;		
		6 ; LABEL SETTINGS		
		7 HTIMI	EQU 0FD9FH	; Hook Jump - Timer
		8 SCRMOD	EQU 0FCAFH	; RAM Storage - Screen Mode
		9 SETWRT	EQU 0053H	; ROM Routine - Set Video

				Write
		10 ;		
D000	3EC3	11 START:	LD A,0C3H	; Value for JUMP instruction
D002	329FFD	12	LD (HTIMI),A	; Load into Hook
D005	210CD0	13	LD HL,CUE	; Address to jump to
D008	22A0FD	14	LD (HTIMI+1),A	; Load into Hook
D00B	C9	15	RET	
		16 ;		
D00C	CD14D0	17 CUE:	CALL CLOCK	; Call CLOCK routine
D00F	F7	18	RST 030H	; Disk delay routine
D010	879C77	19	DEFB 087H,09CH,077H	;-remove if you do not
D013	C9	20		; have a disk drive
		21 ;		
D014	161D0	22 CLOCK:	LD HL,STORE	; Decrease counter
D017	7E	23	LD A,(HL)	;
D018	3D	24	DEC A	;
D019	77	25	LD (HL),A	;
D01A	C0	26	RET NZ	; Return if not ZERO
D01B	3E33	27	LD A,51	; Set new counter
D01D	77	28	LD (HL),A	;
D01E	2162D0	29	LD HL,CLKSTR	; Update - seconds
D021	0603	30	LD B,3	; - minutes
D023	7E	31 CL1:	LD A,(HL)	; - hours
D024	3C	32	INC A	;
D025	27	33	DAA	; Decimal addition
D026	FE69	34	CP 060H	;
D028	3003	35	JR NC,CL2	;
D02A	77	36	LD (HL),A	;
D02B	1805	37	JR PRTCLK	;
D02D	3600	38 CL2:	LD (HL),0	;
D02F	23	39	INC HL	;
D030	10F1	40	DJNZ CL1	;
D032	3AAFFC	41 PRTCLK:	LD A,(SCRMOD)	; Get screen mode
D035	3D	42	DEC A	;

D036	D0	43	RET NC	; Check for screen 0
D037	211F00	44	LD HL,31	;
D03A	CD5300	45	CALL SETWRT	; Set screen address
D03D	2164D0	46	LD HL,CLKSTR+2	; Set pointer to clock
D040	0603	47	LD B,3	; Set counter
D042	7E	48 P1:	LD A,(HL)	;
D043	27	49	DAA	;
D044	F5	50	PUSH AF	; Save value
D045	CB3F	51	SRL A	; Get right digit
D047	CB3F	52	SRL A	;
D049	CB3F	53	SRL A	;
D04B	CB3F	54	SRL A	;
D04D	C630	55	ADD A,48	; Change to ASCII
D04F	D398	56	OUT (098H),A	; Send to screen
D051	F1	57	POP AF	; Return value
D052	E60F	58	AND 1111B	; Get left digit
D054	C630	59	ADD A,48	; Change to ASCII
D056	D398	60	OUT (098H),A	; Send to screen
D058	3E3A	61	LD A,58	; Value for ':'
D05A	2B	62	DEC HL	; Update pointer
D05B	05	63	DEC B	; Update counter
D05C	C8	64	RET Z	; Return if finished
D05D	D398	65	OUT (098H),A	; Send ':' to screen
D05F	18E1	66	JR P1	; Go again
		67 ;		
		68 ; DATA STORAGE		
D061	33	69 STORE:DEFB 51		
D062	000000	70 CLKSTR:DEFB 0,0,0		
D065		71 END:		

Basic Loader

```
10 CLS:CLEAR 200,&HCFFF:DEFINTA-Z:A=&HD000
20 READ A$:IF A$ <> "@" THEN POKE A,
VAL("&H"+A$):A=A+1:GOTO 20
30 PRINT"  INSERT TAPE/DISK TO SAVE PROGRAM"
40 PRINT"         AND PRESS ANY KEY"
50 A$=INPUT$(1):PRINT:PRINT "  SAVING ...."
60 BSAVE"CLOCK",&HD000,A-1
100 DATA 3E,C3,32,9F,FD,21,0C,D0,21,0C,D0,22,A0
,FD,C9,CD
110 DATA 14,D0,F7,87,9C,77,C9,21,61,D0,7E,3D,77
,C0,3E,33
120 DATA 77,21,62,D0,06,03,7E,3C,27,FE,60,30,03
,77,18,05
130 DATA 36,00,23,10,F1,3A,AF,FC,3D,D0,21,1F,00
,CD,53,00
140 DATA 21,64,D0,06,03,7E,27,F5,CB,3F,CB,3F,CB
,3F,CB,3F
150 DATA C6,30,D3,98,F1,E6,0F,C6,30,D3,98,3E,3A
,2B,05,C8
160 DATA D3,98,18,E1,33,00,00,00,@
```

If you do not have a disk drive, change line 110 to -;

```
110 DATA 14,D0,00,00,00,00,C9,21,61,D0,7E,3D,77
,C0,3E,33
```

This program displays a clock in the top right hand corner of the screen, but only when the computer is in screen mode zero. The first part of the program fills the Hook HTIMI with a jump command pointing to a routine called CUE. This routine calls all the things that are using this Hook. In this case, just the two things are being called, the clock routine, and the routine to turn the disk drive motor off after a certain period of time. If you are not using a disk drive, set the four memory locations to zero. In later articles, I will detail more routines that use this Hook.

The clock routine starts by decreasing the first counter, which was initially set to 51. This counter is to measure the passing of one second (The Hook is called every 1/50th of a second). Once a second has passed, the clock counters for the hour, minutes and seconds are updated. Then, if the screen mode is set to zero, the clock will be printed out.

In the next section, I will cover another of the Hook jumps called **HGONE**, and show how new statements can be added to your Basic programs.

Beyond Basic - Part 3

Written By: Tony Cruise

First Published: Micro's Gazette – Issue 000 (November/December 1988)

Introduction

This issue I will explain about the Hook HGONE which can be used to add extra commands to your Basic programs. This eliminates the need to use USR statements which can be confusing to use for people who are not familiar with machine code. It also limits the number of parameters to one.

The Hook HGONE is called by the Basic ROM before each statement is processed. This allows you to add a routine that checks if the next Basic statement is one that you have added. For the ease of checking I will use the '[' character to identify any commands that we add.

The following routine creates two new Basic commands called [BANG and [ZAP. Each time you use these statements they will produce a sound, [BANG an explosion sound and [ZAP a laser firing sound. These new commands can be used in your Basic programs.

e.g.

```
10 PRINT "THIS IS A LASER...":[ZAP
20 FOR A=1 TO 500:NEXT A
30 PRINT "THIS IS AN EXPLOSION...":[BANG
```

Machine Code Program

0000		1 ORIGIN		; Example of Hook HGONE
		2		;
D000		3	ORG 0D000H	
		4		;
		5 HGONE	EQU 0FF43H	; Hook Jump - Basic

				handler
				;
D000	F3	START	DI	
D001	210ED0		LD HL,CHECK	; Address to jump to
D004	2244FF		LD (HGONE+1),HL	; Load into Hook
D007	3EC3		LD A,0C3H	; Value for JUMP
D009	3243FF		LD (HGONE),A	; Load into Hook
D00C	FB		EI	
D00D	C9		RET	
				;
D00E	FE5B		CHECK CP "["	; Is next statement
D010	C0		RET NZ	; one of our commands
D011	F3		DI	;
D012	E5		PUSH HL	; Save pointer
D013	1149D0		LD DE,TABLE	; Table of new commands
D016	0600		LD B,0	; Loop counter
D018	23	LOOP1	INC HL	; Increment pointer
D019	1A		LD A,(DE)	;
D01A	FE00		CP 0	;
D01C	2002		JR NZ,LOOP2	; End of Table?
D01E	1842		JR EXIT	; Yes - Back to Basic
D020	FE2E	LOOP2	CP "."	; End of statement
D022	2015		JR NZ,LOOP3	; No keep going
D024	33		INC SP	; Get rid of old
D025	33		INC SP	; pointer
D026	E5		PUSH HL	; save new pointer
D027	DD2153D0		LD IX,JMPTBL	;
D02B	1600		LD D,0	;
D02D	58		LD E,B	;
D02E	CB23		SLA E	;
D030	DD19		ADD IX,DE	;

D032	DD6E00		LD L,(IX+0)	; Calculate jump
D035	DD6601		LD H,(IX+1)	; address
D038	E9		JP (HL)	;
D039	4E	LOOP3	LD C,(HL)	; Get next character
D03A	13		INC DE	; Set DE for next loop
D03B	B9		CP C	; Match?
D03C	28DA		JR Z,LOOP1	; Yes, go again
D03E	04		INC B	; Next statement
D03F	E1		POP HL	;
D040	E5		PUSH HL	; Restore pointer
D041	1A	LOOP4	LD A,(DE)	;
D042	13		INC DE	; Move DE to next
D043	FE2E		CP "."	; statement
D045	28D1		JR Z,LOOP1	; Loop again
D047	18F8		JR LOOP4	;
				;
D049	42414E47	TABLE	DEFM "BANG."	; Statement table
D04D	2E			
D04E	5A41592E		DEFM "ZAP."	;
D052	00		DEFB 0	;
				;
D053	74D0	JMPTBL	DEFW BANG	; Jump Table
D055	8CD0		DEFW ZAP	;
				;
D057	1A	SOUND	LD A,(DE)	; Get next value
D058	FEFF		CP 255	; End of List?
D05A	C8		RET Z	; Yes - Return
D05B	D3A0		OUT (0A0H),A	; Send value
D05D	13		INC DE	; Increment pointer

D05E	FE07		CP 7	; Is it register 7
D060	1A		LD A,(DE)	;
D061	2006		JR NZ,SNDLP1	; No - Continue
D063	47		LD B,A	;
D064	DBA2		IN A,(0A2H)	; Get current value
D066	E6C0		AND 192	;
D068	80		ADD A,B	; Combine values
D069	D3A1	SNDLP1	OUT (0A1H),A	; Send value
D06B	13		INC DE	; Increment pointer
D06C	18E9		JR SOUND	;
				;
D06E	E1	EXIT	POP HL	; Restore pointer
D06F	7E		LD A,(HL)	; Restore A
D070	33		INC SP	; Get rid of
D071	33		INC SP	; Basic return
D072	FB		EI	;
D073	C9		RET	;
				;
D074	117CD0	BANG	LD DE,BANG1	; Set pointer
D077	CD57D0		CALL SOUND	; Call sound routine
D07A	18F2		JR EXIT	; Exit to Basic
				;
D07C	09100208	BANG1	DEFB 9,16,2,8,3,5,7,40	
D080	03050728			
D084	06140C0A		DEFB 6,20,12,10,13,0,255,255	
D088	0D00FFFF			
				;
D08C	1194D0	ZAP	LD DE,ZAP1	; Set pointer
D08F	CD57D0		CALL SOUND	; Call sound routine
D092	18DA		JR EXIT	; Exit to Basic

		98		;
D094	091002C8	99 ZAP1	DEFB 9,16,2,200,3,0,12,6	
D098	03000C08			
D09C	07380D04	100	DEFB 7,56,13,4,255,255	
D0A0	FFFF			
D0A2		101 END		

Basic Loader

```
10 CLS:CLEAR 200,&HCFFF:DEFINTA-Z:A=&HD000
20 READ A$:IF A$ <> "@" THEN POKE A,
VAL("&H"+A$):A=A+1:GOTO 20
30 PRINT"  INSERT TAPE/DISK TO SAVE PROGRAM"
40 PRINT"          AND PRESS ANY KEY"
50 A$=INPUT$(1):PRINT:PRINT "  SAVING ...."
60 BSAVE"CHECK",&HD000,A-1
100 DATA
F3,21,0E,D0,22,44,FF,3E,C3,32,43,FF,FB,C9,FE,5B
110 DATA
C0,F3,E5,11,49,D0,06,00,23,1A,FE,00,20,02,18,4E
120 DATA
FE,2E,20,15,33,33,E5,DD,21,53,D0,16,00,58,CB,23
130 DATA
DD,19,DD,6E,00,DD,66,01,E9,4E,13,B9,28,DA,04,E1
140 DATA
E5,1A,13,FE,2E,28,D1,18,F8,42,41,4E,47,2E,5A,41
150 DATA
50,2E,00,74,D0,8C,D0,1A,FE,FF,C8,D3,A0,13,FE,07
160 DATA
1A,20,06,47,DB,A2,E6,C0,80,D3,A1,13,18,E9,E1,7E
170 DATA
33,33,FB,C9,11,7C,D0,CD,57,D0,18,F2,09,10,02,08
180 DATA
03,05,07,28,06,14,0C,0A,0D,00,FF,FF,11,94,D0,CD
190 DATA
57,D0,18,DA,09,10,02,C8,03,00,0C,06,07,38,0D,04
200 DATA FF,FF,@
```

Next issue I will cover how to read command line variables and start on the new commands.

Beyond Basic – Part 4

Written By: Tony Cruise

First Published: Micro's Gazette – Issue 002 (March/April 1989)

Introduction

This issue I will start to cover some of the routines that will be used in our extended Basic. We will start off with the new sprite commands.

You can have up to 32 sprites on the screen at once but if you want to move more than about five or six, your program slows down considerably. The routines this issue allow you to specify X and Y velocities for each of the 32 sprites and then they will be moved independently of your Basic program.

I have included an assembler listing explaining how it works as well as a basic loader program for those people who do not have assemblers and a demonstration program.

Machine Code Program

		;	Program to move sprites by velocity	
		;		
D000		ORIGIN	ORG D000H	
		;		
		;	Label settings	
		;		
		HTIMI	EQU FD9FH	; Hook jump - Timer
		SCRMOD	EQU FCAFH	; RAM storage - Screen mode
		SETWRT	EQU 0053H	; ROM routine - Set video write
		SETRD	EQU 0050H	; ROM routine - Set video read
		;		
D000	3EC3	START	LD A,C3H	; Value for JUMP instruction
D002	329FFD		LD (HTIMI),A	; Load into Hook

D005	210CD0		LD HL,QUE	; Address to jump to
D008	22A0FD		LD (HTIMI+1),HL	; Load into Hook
D00B	C9		RET	;
		;		
D00C	CD14D0	QUE	CALL SPRMOV	; Call SPRMOV routine
D00F	F7879C77		DEFB F7H,87H,9CH,77H	; Disk delay routine, remove if
D013	C9		RET	; up do not have a disk drive
		;		
D014	3AAFFC	SPRMOV	LD A,(SCRMOD)	; Get screen mode
D017	FE00		CP 0	;
D019	C8		RET Z	; Make sure not screen 0
D01A	3A47D1		LD A,(MOVFLG)	;
D01D	FE00		CP 0	; Get move flag
D01F	C8		RET Z	;
D020	21001B		LD HL,1B00H	; Return if move set to off
D023	1187D0		LD DE,SPRTBL	;
D026	018000		LD BC,128	;
D029	CD78D0		CALL LDIRVM	; Get sprite table
D02C	2187D0		LD HL,SPRTBL	; Set pointer to sprite table
D02F	0620		LD B,32	; Set loop counter
D031	1107D1		LD DE,SPRVEL	; Set point to velocities
D034	7E	LOOP1	LD A,(HL)	;
D035	FED1		CP 209	; Is the sprite on screen?
D037	281A		JR Z,LOOP2	; No skip
D039	4F		LD C,A	;
D03A	1A		LD A,(DE)	; Get Y velocity
D03B	81		ADD A,C	; Add Y velocity
D03C	FEDC		CP 220	; Off Top of screen
D03E	3804		JR C,LOOP3	; No skip
D040	3EC0		LD A,192	; Yes, correct value
D042	1805		JR LOOP4	;

D044	FEC0	45 LOOP3	CP 192	; Off bottom of screen?
D046	3801	46	JR C,LOOP4	; No skip
D048	AF	47	XOR A	; Yes, correct value
D049	77	48 LOOP4	LD (HL),A	; Store new value
D04A	23	49	INC HL	;
D04B	13	50	INC DE	; Increment pointers
D04C	7E	51	LD A,(HL)	;
D04D	4F	52	LD C,A	;
D04E	1A	53	LD A,(DE)	; Get X velocity
D04F	81	54	ADD A,C	; Add X velocity
D050	77	55	LD (HL),A	; Store new value
D051	2B	56	DEC HL	;
D052	1B	57	DEC DE	; Restore pointers
D053	13	58 LOOP2	INC DE	;
D054	13	59	INC DE	;
D055	23	60	INC HL	;
D056	23	61	INC HL	;
D057	23	62	INC HL	;
D058	23	63	INC HL	; Update pointers
D059	05	64	DEC B	; Decrease loop counter
D05A	20D8	65	JR NZ,LOOP1	; Next loop
D05C	21001B	66	LD HL,1B00H	;
D05F	1187D0	67	LD DE,SPRTBL	;
D062	018000	68	LD BC,128	;
D065	CD69D0	69	CALL LDIRMV	; Save sprite table
D068	C9	70	RET	;
		71 ;		
		72 ;	Move a block of memory from video RAM	
		73 ;		
D069	CD5300	74 LDIRMV	CALL SETWRT	
D06C	1A	75 LP1	LD A,(DE)	
D06D	D398	76	OUT (98H),A	
D06F	13	77	INC DE	
D070	0B	78	DEC BC	
D071	78	79	LD A,B	
D072	B1	80	OR C	

D073	FE00		CP 0	
D075	20F5		JR NZ,LP1	
D077	C9		RET	
		;		
		;	Move a block of memory to video RAM	
		;		
D078	CD5000	LDIRVM	CALL SETRD	
D07B	DB98	LP2	IN A,(98H)	
D07D	12		LD (DE),A	
D07E	13		INC DE	
D07F	0B		DEC BC	
D080	78		LD A,B	
D081	B1		OR C	
D082	FE00		CP 0	
D084	20F5		JR NZ,LP2	
D086	C9		RET	
		;		
		;	Data storage	
		;		
D087		SPRTBL	DEFS 128	
D107		SPRVEL	DEFS 64	
D147	00	MOVFLG	DEFB 0	
		END		

Basic Loader

```
10 CLS:CLEAR 200,&HCFFF:DEFINTA-Z:A=&HD000
20 READ A$:IF A$ <> "@" THEN POKE A,
VAL("&H"+A$):A=A+1:GOTO 20
30 POKE &HD147,0
40 PRINT"  INSERT TAPE/DISK TO SAVE PROGRAM"
50 PRINT"         AND PRESS ANY KEY"
60 A$=INPUT$(1):PRINT:PRINT "  SAVING ...."
70 BSAVE"SPRITE.OBJ",&HD000,&HD147
80 END
100 DATA 3E,C3,32,9F,FD,21,0C,D0,22,A0,FD,C9,CD,14,D0
110 DATA F7,87,9C,77 (or DATA 00,00,00,00 if you
don't have a disk drive)
120 DATA C9,3A,AF,FC,FE,00,C8,3A,47,D1,FE,00,C8,21,00
130 DATA 1B,11,87,D0,01,80,00,CD,78,D0,21,87,D0,06,20
140 DATA 11,07,D1,7E,FE,D1,28,1A,4F,1A,81,FE,DC,38,04
```

```
150 DATA 3E,C0,18,05,FE,C0,38,01,AF,77,23,13,7E,4F,1A
160 DATA 81,77,2B,1B,13,13,23,23,23,23,05,20,D8,21,00
170 DATA 1B,11,87,D0,01,80,00,CD,69,D0,C9,CD,53,00,1A
180 DATA D3,98,13,0B,78,B1,FE,00,20,F5,C9,CD,50,00,DB
190 DATA 98,12,13,0B,78,B1,FE,00,20,F5,C9,@
```

Basic Program Example

```
10 COLOR 15,1,9:SCREEN 2,2:SPRITE$(0) =
STRING$(32,244):DEF FNA(X) = INT(RND(1)*X)+1:A =
RND(-TIME)
20 STOP ON:ON STOP GOSUB 110
30 POKE &HD147,1:FOR A=0 TO 31
40 PUT SPRITE A,(128,96),FNA(15),0
50 XV=FNA(5)-3:IF XV<0 THEN XV=XV+256
60 YV=FNA(5)-3:IF YV<0 THEN YV=YV+256
70 IF XV+YV=0 THEN 50
80 POKE &HD107+A*2,YV:POKE &HD108+A*2,XV:NEXT
90 IF NOT(STRIG(0)) THEN 90 ELSE POKE &HD147,0
100 IF NOT(STRIG(0)) THEN 100 ELSE POLE &HD147,1:GOTO
80
110 POKE &HD147,0:END
```

Type in the machine code loader first and save it to disk or tape. Now type in the Basic example program and save it to tape or disk. Then use BLOAD"SPRITE.OBJ",R to run the machine code program and then RUN the example Basic program.

Next month I will cover the collision testing routines. Bye for now!

Beyond Basic – Part 5

Written By: Tony Cruise

First Published: Micro's Gazette – Issue 003 (May/June 1989)

Introduction

This issue I will start to detail the collision detection routine to go with the automatic sprite routines from last issue. But first here is a list of the conversions for SVI-318/328 to MSX.

Part 1

The SVI-318/328 use the port 8C to change slots. So to change between the RAM and ROM slots use:

ROM to RAM	RAM to ROM
LD A,0FH	LD A,(FE64H)
OUT (88H),A	OUT (8CH),A
IN A,(90H)	
LD (FE64H),A	
AND FDH	
OUT (8CH),A	

Part 2 Onwards

Here is a list of ROM calls, RAM locations and HOOK addresses to use instead of the MSX values.

- HGONE = FF57H,
- HTIMI = FF5AH,
- SCRMOD = FE3AH
- SETWRT = 373CH,
- SETRD = 3747H

Change the following port calls to:

- OUT (98H),A becomes OUT (80H),A
- IN A,(98H) becomes IN A,(84H)

This list will be expanded if necessary, each issue.

Sprite Collision Detection

Now onto this months routine. Our routine will test the collision of one sprite (you specify) with all 31 others. A table of flags will be used to show which sprites the one specified is colliding with. The size of each sprite will be specified by a X and Y with from 0 to 15 (There is no zero width, work out the real value and subtract one). For the routine to work effectively, your sprite shapes should be drawn from the top left hand corner of the sprite shape pattern.

e.g. X width 5, Y width 2

To make the routine easier to understand I have split it into two sections. The section I will show this issue is the actual test routine, that tests whether two specified sprites are colliding and setting the carry flag if so. The values of the registers on entry are:

- HL points to sprite 1 VRAM table location
- DE points to sprite 2 VRAM table location
- B lower 4 bits, y width and top 4 bits, x width for sprite 1
- C lower 4 bits, y width and top 4 bits, x width for sprite 2

Machine Code Program

		;	Subroutine to test the collision of two sprites	
		;		
		;		
		;		
		; Label settings		
		;		
		SETRD	EQU 0050H	; Video read
		;		
C0FA	E5	START	PUSH HL	; Save registers
C0FB	D5		PUSH DE	;
C0FC	C5		PUSH BC	;
C0FD	78		LD A,B	; Get Y velocity 1
C0FE	E60F		AND 15	;

C100	47	LD B,A	;
C101	79	LD A,C	; Get Y velocity 2
C102	E60F	AND 15	;
C104	4F	LD C,A	;
C105	CD55C1	CALL RDVRM	; Get Y1 value
C108	80	ADD A,B	; Add velocity
C109	47	LD B,A	;
C10A	EB	EX DE,HL	; Get Y2 value
C10B	CD55C1	CALL RDVRM	;
C10E	EB	EX DE,HL	;
C10F	B8	CP B	; Hit?
C110	3040	JR NC,NOHIT	; No - Exit loop
C112	EB	EX DE,HL	; Get Y2 value
C113	CD55C1	CALL RDVRM	;
C116	EB	EX DE,HL	;
C117	81	ADD A,C	; Add velocity
C118	4F	LD C,A	;
C119	CD55C1	CALL RDVRM	; Get Y1 velocity
C11C	B9	CP C	; Hit?
C11D	3033	JR NC,NOHIT	; No - Exit loop
C11F	C1	POP BC	; Restore BC
C120	C5	PUSH BC	; Resave BC
C121	23	INC HL	; Increment pointers
C122	13	INC DE	;
C123	CB38	SRL B	; Get X velocity 1
C125	CB38	SRL B	;
C127	CB38	SRL B	;
C129	CB38	SRL B	;
C12B	CB39	SRL C	; Get X velocity 2
C12D	CB39	SRL C	;
C12F	CB39	SRL C	;
C131	CB39	SRL C	;
C133	CD55C1	CALL RDVRM	; Get Y1 value
C136	80	ADD A,B	; Add velocity
C137	47	LD B,A	;
C138	EB	EX DE,HL	; Get Y2 velocity
C139	CD55C1	CALL RDVRM	;
C13C	EB	EX DE,HL	;
C13D	B8	CP B	; Hit?
C13E	3012	JR NC,NOHIT	; No - Exit loop
C140	EB	EX DE,HL	; Get Y2 value

C141	CD55C1		CALL RDVRM	;
C144	EB		EX DE,HL	;
C145	81		ADD A,C	; Add velocity
C146	4F		LD C,A	;
C147	CD55C1		CALL RDVRM	; Get Y1 value
C14A	B9		CP C	; Hit?
C14B	3005		JR NC,NOHIT	; No - Exit loop
C14D	37		SCF	; Set carry flag
C14E	C1	EXIT	POP BC	; Restore registers
C14F	D1		POP DE	;
C150	E1		POP HL	;
C151	C9		RET	; Return from routine
C152	AF	NOHIT	XOR A	; Clear flags
C153	18F9		JR EXIT	; Go to EXIT
C155		;		
C155		;	Subroutine to read a byte from VRAM	
C155		;		
C155	CD5000	RDVRM	CALL SETRD	; Set screen location
C158	D898		IN A,(98H)	; Get value
C15A	C9		RET	;
C15B		;		
		END		

House Keeping Commands

The following commands may be included in programs but are mainly thought of as Housekeeping Commands. They are used to assist you to program. Some like RUN and LIST are essential.

`AUTO [<line number>[,<increment>]]`

Example: AUTO 100,50

AUTO 20

Purpose: To generate a line number automatically after each carriage return [Enter].

AUTO begins numbering at <line number> and increments each subsequent line number by <increment>. The default for both values is 10. If <line number> is followed by a comma but <increment> is not specified, the last increment specified in an auto command is assumed.

If AUTO generates a line number that is already being used, an asterisk (*) is printed after the number to warn the user that any input will replace the existing line. However, typing a carriage return immediately after the asterisk will save the line and generate the next line number.

AUTO is terminated by type Control-C (or Control-[Stop]). The line in which Control-C is typed is not saved. After Control-C is typed, Basic returns to the command level.

`CONT`

Example: CONT

Purpose: To continue program execution after a Control-STOP has been typed, or a STOP or END statement has been executed.

Execution resumes at the point where the break occurred. If the break occurred after a prompt from an INPUT statement, execution continues with the reprinting of the prompt (? Or prompt string).

CONT is usually used in conjunction with STOP for debugging. When execution is stopped, intermediate values may be examined and changed using direct mode statements. Execution may be resumed with CONT or a direct mode GOTO, which resumes execution at a specified line number.

CONT is invalid if the program has been edited during the break. The Can't Continue Error is displayed.

```
DELETE <line number>[-<line number>]
```

Example: DELETE 55-330
DELETE 27

Purpose: To delete program lines.

Basic always returns to command level after a DELETE is executed. If <line number> does not exist an Illegal function call error occurs.

```
KEY <function key #>,<string expression>
```

Example: KEY 1,"FILES"+CHR$(13)

Purpose: To assign new values to the function keys

To set a string to a specified function key. <function key #> must be in the range 1 to 10. <string expression> must be within 15 characters. Any legal string expression may be assigned to a function key.

```
KEY LIST
```

Example: KEY LIST

color	auto
goto	list
run	color 15,4,5

cload"	cont
list .	run

Purpose: To display the full contents of all the function keys.

Thus "color" aligns with key "F1", "auto" with "F2", "goto" with "F3" and so on. Position in the list reflects the key assignments. Note that any control characters assigned to a function key are converted to spaces.

```
LIST/LLIST [<line number][-[<line number?]]]
```

Example: LLIST 100-720
LIST -50

Purpose: To list all or part of the program currently in memory at the terminal or to a printer.

Format 1: If <line number> is omitted, the program is listed beginning at the lowest line number. (Listing is terminated either by the END of the program or by typing control-STOP, the listing may be paused and restarted with the STOP key). If <line number> is included the specified line will be displayed.

Format 2: This format allows the following options:

1. If only the <line number> is specified, that line and all higher numbered lines are listed. LIST 170-
2. If only the second number is specified, all lines from the beginning of the program through to that line are listed. LIST -2110
3. If both numbers are specified, the entire range is listed. LIST 70-3000

```
MERGE "<device descriptor> <file name>"
```

Example: MERGE "CAS:FRED"
MERGE "1:TEMP"

Purpose: MERGE a specified DISK or CASSETTE file into the program currently in memory.

The <file name> is the file name used when the file was saved. The file must be saved in ASCII format. SAVE"1:FRED",A

If any lines in the file being MERGEd have the same line number as lines in the program in memory, the lines from the file will replace the corresponding lines in memory. After the MERGE command, the MERGEd program resides in memory, and BASIC returns to the command level.

If the <file name> is omitted, the next program encountered on Cassette tape is MERGEd. (i.e. MERGE"CAS:"). Control-Z is treated as end-of-file.

Note: MSX Basic uses A and B to identify disk drives e.g. MERGE"A:TEMP".

`NEW`

Example: NEW

Purpose: To delete the program currently in memory and clears all variables.

NEW is entered at command level to clear memory before entering a new program. Basic always returns to the command level after a NEW is executed.

`RENUM [[<new number>[,<old number>[,<increment>]]]`

Example: RENUM 100,200,10
RENUM

Purpose: To RENUMber the program lines.

The <new number> is the first line number to be used in the new sequence. The default is 10. <old number> is the line in the current program where RENUMbering is to begin. The default is the first line of the program. <increment> is the increment to be used in the new sequence. The default is 10.

RENUM also changes all the line number references following GOTO, GOSUB, THEN, ON...GOTO, ON...GOSUB, ERL etc statements to reflect the new line numbers. If a non-existent line number appears after one of these statements, the ERROR message UNDEFINED LINE xxxxx IN yyyyy is printed. The incorrect line number reference (xxxxx) is not changed by RENUM, but line number (yyyyy) may be changed.

Note: RENUM cannot be used to change the order of the program lines (for example, RENUM 15,30 when the program has 3 lines numbered 10,20 and 30) or to create line numbers greater than 65529.

`RUN [<line number>]`

Example: RUN 800
RUN

Purpose: To execute the program currently in memory. See RUN <file name> as well.

If <line number> is specified, execution will begin on that line. Otherwise, execution will begin at the lowest line number. Basic always returns to command level after a RUN is executed.

`TRON/TROFF`

Example:

```
TRON
Ok
LIST
10 K=10
20 FOR J=1 TO 2
30 L=K+10
```

```
40 PRINT J;K;L
50 K=K+10
60 NEXT J
70 END
Ok
RUN
C10C20C30C40 1 10 20
C50C60C30C40 2 20 30
C50C60C70
Ok
TROFF
Ok
```

Purpose: To trace the execution of program statements.

As an aid in debugging, the TRON statement, executed in either direct or indirect mode, enables a trace flag that prints each line number of the program as it is executed. The numbers appear in square brackets. The trace flag is disabled with the TROFF statement, or when a new command is executed.

WARNING: unusual results are printed in SCREEN 1 and SCREEN 2. (Screens 2 and 3 in MSX Basic).

```
WIDTH <integer expression>
```

Example:

```
WIDTH 80
WIDTH 39
```

Purpose: To set the printed line WIDTH in number of characters for the terminal.

The line width is set at the terminal. Legal widths for Spectravideo Basic in SCREEN 0 are 39 or 30 however WIDTH 80 may be selected only if the 80 Column Card is installed. MSX Basic allows any value from 1 to 40 (or 80 if an 80 Column Card or MSX 2 video chip is installed) in SCREEN 0 or SCREEN 1.

Loading and Saving Programs

Basic stores programs in three different ways, they are explained below. Your programs may be stored on Cassette, or either of the attached disk drives. The following three examples show how this is done.

CSAVE"FRED" Tells Basic to save a program on Cassette.

CLOAD"FRED" Tells Basic to load a program from Cassette.

SAVE"CAS:FRED",A "CAS:" tells Basic to save a program on Cassette, with the 'A' indicating that the program be stored in ASCII format.

LOAD"1:FRED" "1:" Tells Spectravideo Basic to load a program from the first disk drive.

LOAD"A:FRED" "A:" Tells MSX Basic to load a program from the first disk drive.

BLOAD"2:FRED" "2:" Tells Spectravideo Basic to load a machine code program from the second disk drive.

BLOAD"B:FRED" "B:" Tells MSX Basic to load a machine code program from the second disk drive.

```
BLOAD "<device descriptor>[<file name>]" ,[,R]
[,<offset>]
```

Example: BLOAD"CAS:GAME",R,&H8800
BLOAD"CAS:",R

Purpose: To load a machine language program from a specified device into memory.

If [,R] option is specified, after the loading, the program begins execution automatically from the address which was specified at BSAVE.

The loaded machine language program will be stored at the memory location which was specified at BSAVE. If <offset> is specified all addresses which were specified at BSAVE are offset by that value.

BLOAD does not perform an address range check. Thus it is possible to BLOAD over Basic's stack, programs or variable area.

```
BSAVE "<device descriptor><file name>",<top address>,<end address>[,<execution address>]
```

Example: BSAVE"2:GAME",&H8000,&HD3FF,&H8800 (SVI)
BSAVE"B:GAME",&H8000,&HD3FF,&H8800 (MSX)
BSAVE"BUNNY",&H8500,&H8FFF

Purpose: To save a memory image at the specified memory location to the specified device.

The <top address> specified the starting location of the program.

The <end address> specifies the end location of the program.

The <execution address> specifies the address to begin execution of the program if the [,R] option is used with BLOAD. If <execution address> is omitted, <top address> is regarded as the execution address.

```
CLOAD["<file name>"]
```

Example: CLOAD"CIRCLE"
CLOAD

Purpose: To load a program from Cassette.

If it is a screen image, screen mode is forced to the proper mode. If it is a Basic program, the current program residing in memory is erased.

```
CLOAD?
```

Example: CLOAD?

Purpose: To verify the program just saved.

The program in memory is compared to the program on Cassette and if there are any difference an error is printed. This is a very useful command as your Basic program is not cleared from memory.

```
CSAVE "<file name>"[,S] (SVI Basic)
CSAVE "<file name>"[,n] (MSX Basic)
```

Example: CSAVE"ADDER"
CSAVE"PICTURE",S (SVI)

Purpose: To save a Basic program or screen image (SVI only) to Cassette.

CSAVE is used to save a Basic program efficiently and quickly onto a Cassette.

In SVI Basic if the [,S] option is included, then an image of the current screen is saved on Cassette. This option saves all 16k of VRAM including the current screen mode.

In MSX Basic if the [,n] option is included the program is saved at the baud rate associated with the value used. A value of 0 will save the program at 1200 baud and a value of 1 will save the program at 2400 baud. If no baud rate is specified then the program will be saved at the current baud rate (Set using the SCREEN statement). When the computer is first switched on the baud rate defaults to 1200 baud.

```
LOAD "[<device descriptor>]<file name>"[,R]
```

Example: LOAD"1:TEST" (SVI)
LOAD"A:TEST" (MSX)
LOAD"CAS:ANGLE",R

Purpose: To load a Basic program file from a specified device.

LOAD closes all open files and deletes all variables and program lines currently in memory before it loads the designated program. However, if the [,R] option is used with LOAD, the program is run after it is loaded, and all open data files are kept open. Thus, LOAD with the [,R] option may be used to chain several programs (or segments of the same program). Information may be passed between programs using their Disk Data files.

```
RUN "[<device descriptor>][<file name>]"[,R]
```

Example: RUN"1LRUN" (SVI)
RUN"A:RUN" (MSX)
RUN"NEXT"
RUN"CAS:"

Purpose: To LOAD and execute a program.

RUN closes all open files and deletes the current contents of memory before LOADing the designated program. However, with the [,R] option, all data files remain open.

If this command is used with the Cassette system the program to be loaded must have been SAVEd not CSAVEd before hand.

```
SAVE "[<device descriptor>]<file name>"[,A]
```

Example: SAVE"1:CHIP",A (SVI)
SAVE"A:CHIP",A (MSX)
SAVE"ERIC"

Purpose: To save a Basic program on Disk or Cassette and optionally in ASCII format.

Use the [,A] option when using Disk to SAVE the file in ASCII format. Otherwise Basuc saves the file on Disk in compressed binary format. ASCII format takes up more space on Disk, but some Disk access requires that files be in ASCII format. For instance, the MERGE command requires an ASCII format file.

When using Cassette the SAVE command always saves the program in ASCII format.

Basic Commands

BEEP

Example: BEEP

Purpose: To generate a BEEP sound

The BEEP statement sounds the speaker of the Television set at approximately 1kHz for ¼ of a second.

CALL <name>[<list of arguments>} (MSX Basic Only)

Example: CALL SYSTEM
CALL COMHELP

Purpose: To call a subroutine located in a plug in ROM cartridge or to call a machine specific extended function.

CIRCLE (<coordinate specifier>), <radius> [,<colour>] [,<start angle>] [,<end angle>] [,<aspect ratio>]

Example: CIRCLE STEP(10,50),20
CIRCLE(90,100),50,3,,,1/12

Purpose: To draw an ellipse with a centre and radius as indicated by the first of its arguments.

The (<coordinate specifier>) specified the coordinates for the centre of the circle on the screen. For the detail of <coordinate specifier> see the description in the PUT SPRITE statement.

The <colour> defaults to the foreground colour.

The <start angle> and <end angle> parameters are radian arguments between 0 and 2 x PI, which allow you to specify where drawing of the ellipse will begin and end. If the start angle is negative the ellipse will be connected to the centre point with a line, and the angle will be treated as if it were positive. Note: This is different to adding 2 x PI.

The <aspect ratio> is for horizontal and vertical ratio of the ellipse.

```
CLEAR [<string space>[,<highest location>]]
```

Example:	CLEAR 500 CLEAR 1000,&HE800
Purpose:	To set all variables to zero, all string variables to null and close all open files, also optionally to set the end of memory.

<string space> sets space for string variables. Default size is 200.

<highest location> is used to set the highest memory location available for use by Basic.

```
CLICK [ON][OFF] (SVI Basic only - see SCREEN for
MSX Basic)
```

Example:	CLICK ON CLICK OFF
Purpose:	To turn on and off the CLICK sound.

The CLICK sound is an audible feedback through the Television speaker when a key is pressed. This is very useful on the SVI-318 with it's rubber keys.

```
CLS
```

Example:	CLS
Purpose:	To clear the screen.

The CLS statement is valid in all the screen modes.

```
COLOR [<foreground colour>][,<background colour>][,<border colour>]
```

Example: COLOR 8
COLOR 3,10,14

Purpose: To define the color.

The default colours are 15,4,5. The argument can be in the range of 0-15. The actual colours corresponding to each value are as follows:

0 = transparent	8 = medium red
1 = black	9 = light red
2 = medium green	10 = dark yellow
3 = light green	11 = light yellow
4 = dark blue	12 = dark green
5 = light blue	13 = magenta
6 = dark red	14 = grey
7 = cyan	15 = white

```
DATA <list of constants>
```

Example: DATA 1,7,&H3F,257,458,&O3,0,1,9
DATA "PETER","MARK",7,5300,"HELLO"

Purpose: To store the numeric and/or string constants that are accessed by a program's READ statement(s).

DATA statements are non-executable and may be placed anywhere in the program. A DATA statement may contain as many constants as will fit on a line separated by commas, and any number of DATA statements may be used in a program. The READ statements access the DATA statements in order (i.e. by line numbers) and the DATA contained there may be thought of as one continuous list of items, regardless of how many items are on a line or where the lines are placed in a program.

The list of constants may contain numeric constants in any format i.e. fixed point, floating point or integer. No numeric expressions are allowed in the list. String constants in DATA statements must be surrounded by double quotation marks only if they contain commas, colons or significant leading or trailing spaces. Otherwise quotation marks are not needed.

The variable type given in the READ statement must agree with the corresponding constant in the DATA statement. DATA statements may be read from the beginning or specified line by the use of the RESTORE statement.

```
DEFDBL <range(s) of letters>
DEFINT <range(s) of letters>
DEFSNG <range(s) of letters>
DEFSTR <range(s) of letters>
```

Example: DEFINT A-Z
DEFSNG C,D,L-N

Purpose: To declare variable types as Double Precision (DBL), Integer (INT), Single Precision (SNG) or String (STR).

DEFDBL/INT/SNG/STR statements declare that the variable names neginning with the letters specified will be that type of variable. However a type declaration character always takes precedence over a DEFxxx statement in the typing of a variable. See Program Variables for details.

```
DEFN <name>[(<parameter list>)] = <function
definition>
```

Example: DEF FNG(X)=X^2+X
DEF FNB(X,Y,Z)=X*9+Y*4-SIN(Z)

Purpose: To define and name a function that is written by the user.

<name> mist be a legal variable name. This name preceded by FN becomes the name of the function. The <parameter list> is comprised of those variable names in the function definition that are to be

replaced when the function is called. The items in the list are separated by commas. The <function definition> is an expression that performs the operation of the function. It is limited to one line. Variable names that appear in this expression server only to define the function. A variable name used in a function definition may or may not appear in the parameter list. If it does, the value of the parameter is supplied when the function is called. Otherwise the current value of the variable is used.

The variables in the parameter list represent a one to one basis, the argument variables or values that will be given in the function call.

If a type is specified in the function name, the value of the expression is forced to that type before it is returned to the calling statement. If a type is specified in the function name and the argument does not match, a type mismatch error occurs.

A DEF FN statement must be executed before the function it defines may be called. If a function is called before it has been defined an undefined user function error occurs. DEF FN is illegal in the direct mode.

```
DEFUSR [<digit>] = <integer expression>
```

Example: DEFUSR 0=&H8800
DEFUSR 7=1000

Purpose: To specify the starting address of an assembly language subroutine.

The <digit> may be any digit from 0-9. The digit corresponds to the number of the user routine whose address is being specified. If <digit> is omitted, DEFUSR 0 is assumed. The value of <integer expression> is the starting address of the USR routine.

Any number of DEFUSR statements may appear in the program to redefine subroutine starting addresses. Thus allowing access to as many subroutines as necessary.

`DIM <list of subscripted variables>`

Example: DIM A(9)
DIM AZ$(5,7),P(33),M(9,5,1)

Purpose: To specify the maximum values for array variable subscripts and allocate storage accordingly.

If any variable name is used without a DIM statement, the maximum value of it's subscripts is assumed to be 10. If a subscript is used that is greater than the maximum specified then a subscript out of range error occurs. The minimum value for a subscript is always 0.

`DRAW <string expression>`

Example: DRAW "u714g8f14bm100,100a3"
DRAW A$

Purpose: To draw figures according to the graphic macro language.

The graphic macro language commands are contained in the expression string. The string defines an object, which is drawn when Basic executes the DRAW statement. During execution, Basic examines the value of the string and interprets single letter commands from the contents of the string. These commands are detailed below:

The following movement commands begin movement from the last point referenced. After each command, last point referenced is the last point the command draws.

U n	Move up
D n	Move down
L n	Move left
R n	Move right

E n	Move diagonally up and right
F n	Move diagonally down and right
G n	Move diagonally down and left
H n	Move diagonally up and left

The n in each the preceding commands indicates the distance to move. The number of points is n times the scaling factor (set by the S command).

M x,y	Moves absolute or relative. If x has a plus sign or a minus sign in front of it, it is relative. Otherwise it is absolute.

Note: In SVI Basic a bug causes an error if you use a negative sign for a relative move command. This can be overcome by using the variable inclusion command X (see below).

The aspect ratio of the screen is one. So eight horizontal points are equal in length to 8 vertical points.

The following two prefix commands may precede any of the above movement commands.

B	Moves but doesn't plot any points
N	Moves but returns to the original position when finished

The following commands are also available:

A n	Sets the angle to n. n may range from 0 to 3, where 0 is 0 degrees, 1 is 90, 2 is 180 and 3 is 270.

```
            0

            :

1           +           3

            :
```

C n — Sets the colour n. n may range from 0 to 15

S n — Sets the scale factor. The n may range from 0 to 255. N divided by 4 is the scale factor. For example, if n=1, then the scale factor is ¼. The scale factor multiplied by the distance given with the U,D,L,R,E,F,G,H and relative M commands gives the actual distance moved. The default value is 0, which means 'no-scaling' (i.e. same as S4)

X <string variable>

Executes a substring. This allows you to execute a second string from within a string.

Example:

```
A$ = "D30L40U20"
DRAW"BM60,70D50XA$;"
```

In all these commands, the n,x or y arguments can be a constant like 45 or it can be a variable '=<variable>;' where <variable> is the name of numeric variable. The semi-colon (;) is required when you use a variable this way, or in the X command.

Otherwise, a semi-colon is optional between commands. Spaces are ignored in a string. For example, you could use variables in a move command this way:

```
X1-=50:S1=99

DRAW"M+=X1;-=S1"
```

The X command can be very useful part of DRAW, because you can define a part of an object separately from the entire object and also you can use X to draw a string of commands more than 255 characters long.

END

Example: END

Purpose: To terminate program execution, close all files and return to command level.

The END statement may be placed anywhere in the program to terminate execution. Unlike the STOP statement, END does not cause a BREAK message to be printed. An END statement at the end of a program is optional. (But good programming practice).

```
ERASE <list of array variables>
```

Example: ERASE A
ERASE A,M,M1,F4

Purpose: To eliminate arrays from a program.

Arrays may be redimensioned after the are ERASEd, or the previously allocated array space may be used for other purposes. If an attempt is made to redimension an array without first ERASEing it, a Redimensioned array error occurs.

```
ERROR <integer expression>
```

Example: ERROR 5
ERROR 170 (User defined)

Purpose: To simulate the occurrence of an error or to allow error codes to be defined by the user.

The value of <integer expression> must be greater than 0 and less than 255. If the value of <integer expression> equals an error code already in use by Basic, the ERROR statement will simulate the occurrence of that error and the corresponding error message will be printed.

To define your own error code use a value that is greater than any used by Basic for it's error codes. Refer to a list of error codes and messages in Appendix A. This user defined error code may be conveniently handled in an error trap routine.

Example:

```
10 ON ERROR GOTO 1000
.
.
120 IF A$="Y"THEN ERROR 250
.
.
1000 IF ERR=250 THEN INPUT"Sure ";A$
.
.
```

If an ERROR statement specified a code for which no error message has been defined, Basic responds with the message Unprintable error. Execution of an ERROR statement for which there is no error trap routine causes the same message to be printed and execution stops.

`FOR <variable> = x TO y [STEP] z`

Example:

```
FOR A=1 TO 7000
FOR LOOP = 88 TO 7 STEP -.5
```

Purpose: To allow a series of instructions to be performed in a loop for a given number of times.

The <variable> is used as a counter. The first numeric expression (x) is the initial value of the counter. The second numeric expression (x) is the initial value of the counter. The second numeric expression (y) is the final value of the counter. The program lines following the FOR statement are executed until the NEXT statement is encountered. Then the counter is incremented by the amount specified by the STEP. A check is performed to see if the value of the counter is now greater than the final value (y). If not Basic branches back to the statement after the FOR statement and the process is repeated. If it is greater execution continues with the statement following the NEXT statement. This is a FOR ... NEXT loop. If STEP is not specified the increment is assumed to be one.

If STEP is negative, the final value of the counter is set to be less than the initial value. The counter is decremented each time through the loop and the loop is executed until the counter is less than the final value (y).

The body of the loop is executed at least once if the initial value of the loop times the sign of the STEP exceeds the final value times the sign of the STEP.

FOR ... NEXT loops may be nested, that is, a FOR ... NEXT loop may be placed within context of another FOR ... NEXT loop. When loops are nested, each loop must have a unique variable name as it's counter. The NEXT statement for the inside loop must appear before that of the outside loop. If nested loops have the same end point, a single NEXT statement may be used for all of them.

`GET [(<X1,Y1>)-(<X2,Y2>),] <array name>`

Example:	GET (25,30)-(100,100),F GET S
Purpose:	To read points from the graphic screen.

Points may be read from the entire Graphic Screen or from a defined area of the Graphic Screen. The Array must be a dimensioned large enough to hold the data.

`GOSUB <line number>`

Example:	GOSUB 5000 GOSUB 10
Purpose:	To branch to a subroutine beginning at <line number>

The <line number> is the first line of a subroutine. A subroutine may be called any number of times in a program and a subroutine may be called from within another subroutine. Such nesting of subroutines is limited only by available memory.

```
GOTO <line number>
```

Example: GOTO 900
GOTO 8800

Purpose: To branch unconditionally out of normal program sequence to a specified <line number>

If <line number> is an executable statement, that statement and those following are executed. If it is a non-executable statement, execution proceeds at the first executable statement encountered after <line number>.

```
IF <expression> THEN <statement(s)>[:<line
number> [ELSE <statement(s)>[:<line number>]]]
IF <expression> GOTO <line number> [ELSE
<statement(s)>[: <line number>]]
```

Example: IF A<E OR SIN(9)=T THEN PRINT "HELLO" ELSE 500
IF 45<H GOTO 5

Purpose: To make a decision regarding program flow based on the result returned by an expression.

If the result of <expression> is not zero, the THEN or GOTO clause is executed. THEN may be followed by either a line number for branching or one or more statements to be executed.

GOTO is always follows by a line number.

If the result of <expression> is zero, the THEN or GOTO clause is ignored and the ELSE clause, if present, is executed. Execution continues with the next executable statement.

IF .. THEN .. ELSE statements may be nested. Nesting is limited only by the length of the line (255). If the statement does not contain the same number of ELSE and THEN clauses, each ELSE is matched with the closest unmatched THEN.

e.g. IF G=J THEN IF J=C THEN PRINT "G=C" ELSE PRINT "G<>C"

This will not print "G<>C" when G<>J. If will print "G<>C" when G=J and J<>C.

If an IF .. THEN statement if followed by a line number in the direct mode, an Undefined line error results unless a statement with the specified line number had previously been entered in the indirect mode.

```
INPUT ["<prompt string>";]<list of variables>
```

Example: INPUT "WHAT IS YOUR ANSWER";A$
INPUT A,H,S1,S$,H$(9)

Purpose: To allow input from the keyboard during program execution.

When an INPUT statement is encountered, program execution pauses and a question mark is printed to indicate the program is waiting for data. If "<prompt string>" is included the string is printed before the question mark. The required data is then entered at the keyboard.

The data that is entered is assigned to the variable(s) given in <variable list>. The number of data items supplied must be the same as the number of variables in the list. Data items are separated by commas.

The names in the <list of variables> may be numeric or string variable names (including subscripted variables). The type of each data item that is inputted must agree with the type specified by the variable name. (Strings inputted to an INPUT statement need not be surrounded by quotation marks).

Responding to INPUT with the wrong type of value (string instead of numeric etc) causes the message ?Redo from start to be printed. No assignment of input values are made until an acceptable response is given.

e.g.

```
LIST
10 INPUT "A and B";A,B
20 PRINT A+B
Ok
RUN
A and B? 10,hello
?Redo from start
A and B? 10,20
30
Ok
```

Responding to INPUT with too many items causes the message ?Extra ignored to be printed and the next statement to be executed.

e.g.

```
LIST
10 INPUT "A and B";A,B
20 PRINT A+B
Ok
RUN
A and B? 10,20,30
?Extra ignored
30
Ok
```

Responding to INPUT with too few items causes two question marks to be printed and a wait for the next data item.

e.g

```
LIST
10 INPUT "A and B";A,B
20 PRINT A+B
Ok
RUN
A and B? 10 (10 was typed by user)
```

?? 20 (20 was typed by user)
30
Ok

Escape INPUT by pressing the [CTRL] and [C] or the [CTRL] and [Stop] keys simultaneously. Basic returns to the command level and displays Ok. Typing CONT resumes execution at the INPUT statement.

INTERVAL ON/OFF/STOP

Example: INTERVAL ON
INTERVAL STOP

Purpose: To activate/deactivate trapping of the time interval in a Basic program.

An INTERVAL ON statement must be executed to activate trapping of the time interval. After the INTERVAL ON statement, if a line number is specified previously in the ON INTERVAL GOSUB statement then every time Basic starts a new statement it will check the time interval. If so it will perform a GOSUB to the line number specified in the ON INTERVAL GOSUB statement.

If an INTERVAL OFF statement has been executed, no trapping takes place and the event is not remembered even if it does take place.

If an INTERVAL STOP statement has been executed, no trapping will take place, but if the timer interrupt occurs, this is remembered so an immediate trap will take place when INTERVAL ON is executed.

KEY (<function key #>) ON/OFF/STOP

Example: KEY (1) ON
KEY (7) OFF

Purpose: To activate/deactivate trapping of the specified function key in a Basic program.

A KEY(n) ON statement must be executed to activate trapping of a function key. After a KEY(n) ON statement, if a line number is specified in the ON KEY GOSUB statement, then every time Basic starts a new statement it will check to see if the specified key is pressed. If so it will perform a GOSUB to the line number specified in the ON KEY GOSUB statement.

If a KEY(n) OFF statement has been executed, no trapping takes place and the event is not remembered even if it does take place.

If a KEY(n) STOP statement has been executed, no trapping will take place, but if the specified key is pressed this is remembered so an immediate trap will take place when KEY(n) ON is executed.

KEY(n) ON is not effected by whether the function key values are displayed at the bottom of the console or not.

```
[LET] <variable> = <expression>
```

Example: LET Y = 66 + 7*SIN(9)
T1 = U

Purpose: To assign a value of an expression to a variable.

Notice the word LET is optional i.e. the equal sign is sufficient when assigning an expression to a variable name.

```
LINE [(coordinate specifier<)]-(<coordinate
specifier>)[,<colour>][,<B[F]>]
```

Example: LINE (10,10)-(100,100),6,BF
LINE STEP(30,70)-STEP(10,10)
LINE –(50,50),4

Purpose: To draw a line connecting two specified coordinates or from the current graphic position to a specified point.

For the detail of the <coordinate specifier>, see the description at the PUT SPRITE statement.

The current graphic position is changed to the end position of the line.

If 'B' is specified, a rectangle is drawn.

If 'BF' is specified, a filled rectangle is drawn.

`LINE INPUT ["<prompt string>";]<string variable>`

Example: LINE INPUT "NAME";A$
LINE INPUT PT$

Purpose: To input an entire line (up to 254 characters) to a string variable, without the use of delimiters.

The prompt string is a string literal that is printed at the console before input is accepted. A question mark is not printed, unless it is part of the prompt string. All input from the end of the prompts to the carriage return is assigned to <string variable>.

`LOCATE [<x>][,<y>][,<cursor display switch>]`

Example: LOCATE 10,10,0
LOCATE 5

Purpose: To locate the character position for PRINT on the screen. In MSX Basic LOCATE does not position the cursor in SCREEN 2 or SCREEN 3 (See PSET, PRESET, LINE or DRAW)

<cursor display switch> can only be specified in text mode. (0 in SVI Basic, 0 or 1 in MSX Basic)

0 : disable the cursor display
1 : enable the cursor display

```
LPRINT [<list of expressions>]
LPRINT USING <string expression>;<list of
expressions>
```

Example: LPRINT A$
LPRINT "HELLO"
LPRINT USING "$###.##";666.093

Purpose: To print data to the printer.

See PRINT and PRINT USING statements later in the manual for more details.

```
MID$ (<string exp. 1>, n[,m]) = <string exp. 2>
```

Example: MID$(A$, 6, 9) = D$
MID$(D$,2) = "GOOD"

Purpose: To replace a portion of one string with another string.

The characters in <string exp. 1>, beginning at position n, are replaced by the characters in <string exp. 2>. The optional [,m] refers to the number of characters from <string exp. 2> that will be used in the replacement. The replacement of characters never goes beyond the original length of <string exp. 1>.

```
MOTOR [ON/OFF]
```

Example: MOTOR ON
MOTOR OFF
MOTOR

Purpose: To enable/disable the motor of an attached cassette drive.

ON/OFF changes the status of the cassette motor switch. If neither are specified then the state of the motor is toggled.

```
NEXT [<variable>][,<variable> …]
```

Example: NEXT
NEXT Y,K,H

Purpose: To denote the end of a FOR .. NEXT loop.

The variable(s) in the NEXT statement may be omitted, in which case the NEXT statement will match the most recent FOR statement. If a NEXT statement is encountered before it's corresponding FOR statement a NEXT without FOR error message is issued and execution is terminated.

```
ON ERROR GOTO <line number>
```

Example: ON ERROR GOTO 1000
ON ERROR GOTO 0

Purpose: To enable error trapping and specify the first line of the error handling subroutine.

Once error trapping has been enabled all errors detected, including direct mode errors (e.g. SYNTAX errors), will cause a jump to the specified error handling subroutine. If <line number> does not exist, an Undefined line number error results. To disable error trapping, execute an ON ERROR GOTO 0. Subsequent errors will print an error message and halt execution.

An ON ERROR GOTO 0 statement that appears in an error trapping subroutine causes Basic to stop and print the error that caused the trap. It is recommended that all error trapping subroutines execute an ON ERROR GOTO 0 if an error is encountered for which there is no recovery action.

If an error occurs during execution of an error handling subroutine, the Basic error message is printed and execution terminates. Error trapping does not occur within the error handling subroutine.

```
ON <expression> GOSUB <list of line numbers>
ON <expression> GOTO <list of line numbers>
```

Example: ON I GOSUB 60,70,80,90,300
ON U-7 GOTO 1000,1100,1200,1300,1200,1100

Purpose: To branch to one of several specified line numbers, depending on the value returned when an expression is evaluated.

The value of <expression> determines which line number in the list will be used for branching. For example, if the value is three, the third line number in the list will be the destination of the branch. If the value is non-integer, the fractional portion is discarded.

In the ON ... GOSUB statement, each line number in the list must be the first line number of a subroutine.

If the value of <expression> is zero or greater than the number of items in the list (but less then or equal to 255), Basic continues with the next executable statement. If the value of <expression> is negative or greater then 255, an Illegal function call error occurs.

```
ON INTERVAL = <time interval> GOSUB <line
number>
```

Example: ON INTERVAL = 6000 GOSUB 1300
ON INTERVAL = I/60 GOSUB 7000

Purpose: To setup a line number for Basic to trap to on time intervals.

Generates a timer interrupt every <time interval>/60 seconds.

When the trap occurs an automatic INTERVAL STOP is executed so received traps can never take place. The RETURN from the trap routine will automatically do an INTERVAL ON unless an explicit INTERVAL OFF has been performed inside the trap routine.

Event trapping does not take place when Basic is not executing a program. When an error trap (resulting from an ON ERROR statement) takes place this automatically disables all traps (including ERROR, STRIG, STOP, SPRITE, INTERVAL and KEY).

ON KEY GOSUB <list of line numbers>

Example: ON KEY GOSUB 4000,4100,4200
ON KEY GOSUB 100,200,300,400,500,600,700,800

Purpose: To setup a list of line numbers for Basic to call when a function key is pressed.

When a function key is pressed and the subroutine called, an automatic KEY(n) STOP is executed so further received key presses cannot take place. The RETURN from the subroutine will automatically do a KEY(n) ON unless an explicit KEY(n) OFF has been performed inside the routine.

Event trapping does not take place when Basic is not executing a program. When an error trap (resulting from an ON ERROR statement) takes place this automatically disables all trapping, including ERROR, STRIG, STOP, SPRITE, INTERVAL and KEY.

ON SPRITE GOSUB <line number>

Example: ON SPRITE GOSUB 700
ON SPRITE GOSUB 1000

Purpose: To setup a line number for Basic to jump to when two sprites coincide.

When the trap occurs an automatic SPRITE STOP is executed so any further sprite collisions cannot take place during the trap routine. The RETURN from the trap routine will automatically do a SPRITE ON unless an explicit SPRITE OFF has been performed inside the trap routine.

Event trapping does not take place when Basic is not executing a program. When an error trap (result from an ON ERROR statement) takes place this automatically disables all trapping, including ERROR, STRIG, STOP, SPRITE, INTERVAL and KEY.

ON STOP GOSUB <line number>

Example: ON STOP GOSUB 700
ON STOP GOSUB 30

Purpose: To setup a line number for Basic to jump to when the [CTRL] and [STOP] keys are pressed at the same time.

When the trap occurs an automatic STOP STOP is executed so received traps can never take place. The RETURN from the trap routine will automatically do a STOP ON unless an explicit STOP OFF has been performed inside the trap routine.

Event trapping does not take place when Basic is not executing a program. When an error trap (result from an ON ERROR statement) takes place this automatically disables all trapping, including ERROR, STRIG, STOP, SPRITE, INTERVAL and KEY.

The user must be very careful when using this statement. For example, the following program cannot be aborted. The only way left is to reset the system! (Turn it OFF & ON).

e.g.

```
10 ON STOP GOSUB 40
20 STOP ON
30 GOTO 30
40 RETURN
```

ON STRIG GOSUB <list of line numbers>

Example: ON STRIG GOSUB ,200,,400
ON STRIG GOSUB 9000

Purpose: To setup a line number for Basic to jump to when the trigger button is pressed.

When the trap occurs an automatic STRIG STOP is executed so received traps can never take place. The RETURN from the trap routine will automatically do a STRIG ON unless an explicit STRIG OFF has been performed inside the trap routine.

Event trapping does not take place when Basic is not executing a program. When an error trap (result from an ON ERROR statement) takes place this automatically disables all trapping, including ERROR, STRIG, STOP, SPRITE, INTERVAL and KEY.

`OUT <port number>, <integer expression>`

Example: OUT &H34,0
OUT 255,255

Purpose: To send a byte to a machine output port.

See port map in Appendix B.

The <port number> and <integer expression> are in the range 0 to 255. <integer expression> is the data (byte) to be transmitted.

`PAINT (<coordinate specifier>)[,<paint colour>]`

Example: PAINT (100,100),6
PAINT STEP(10,50),11

Purpose: To fill in an arbitrary graphics figure of the specified fill colour starting at <coordinate specifier>.

For detail of the <coordinate specifier>, see the description at the PUT SPRITE statement.

PAINT does not allow <coordinate specifier> to be off the screen.

<paint colour> is the colour the screen will be painted until points of <paint colour> are encountered.

```
PLAY <string exp for voice 1>[,<string exp for voice 2>][,<string exp for voice 3>]
```

Example: PLAY A$,B$,C$
PLAY "M0909S4T255O3ADA#FFBAC"

Purpose: To play music according to the music macro language.

PLAY implements a concept similar to DRAW by embedding a "music macro language" into a character string. <string exp for voice n> is a string expression consisting of single character music commands. When a null string is specified the voice channel remains silent.

The single character commands in play are:

A to G — with option #, + or -
Plays the indicated note in the current octave. A number sign (#) or plus sign (+) afterwards indicates a sharp, a minus sign (-) indicates a flat. The #, + or – is not allowed unless it corresponds to a black key on a piano. For example, B# is an invalid note.

O n — Octave. Sets the current octave for the following notes. There are 8 octaves, numbered 1 to 8. Each octave goes from C to B. Octave 4 is the default octave.

N n — Plays note n. n may range from 0 to 96. n = 0 means rest. This is an alternative way of selecting notes besides specifying the octave (On) and the note name (A-G). The C of octave 4 is note 36.

L n Sets the length of the following notes. The actual note length is 1/n. n may range from 1 to 64. The following table may help explain this:

Length Equivalent	
L1	Whole Note
L2	Half Note
L3	One of a triplet of three half notes (1/3 of a 4 beat measure)
L4	Quarter note
L5	One of a Quintuplet (1/5 of a measure)
L6	One of a Quarter note Triplet
.	
.	
L64	Sixty-Forth note

The length may also follow the note when you want to change the length only for the note. For example, A16 is equivalent to L16A. The default is 4.

P n Pause (rest). n may range from 1 to 64 and figures the length of the pause in the same way as L (Length). The default is 4.

. (Dot or period). After note, causes the note to be played as a dotted note. That is, it's length is multiplied by 3/2. More than one dot may appear after the note and the length is adjusted accordingly. For example, "A..." will play 27/8 as long, etc. Dots may also appear after the pause (P) to scale the pause length in the same way.

T n Tempo. Sets the number of quarter notes in a minute. N may range from 32 to 255. The default is 120.

V n Volume. Sets the volume of output. n may range from 0 to 15. The default is 8.

M n Modulation. Sets period of the envelope. n may range from 1 to 65535. The default is 8.

S n Shape. Sets shape of envelope. n may range from 1 to 15. The default is 1. The patterns set by this command are as follows:

```
0,1,2,3,9          \
                    \
                     ------------------------------------------------------------

4,5,6,7,15          /!
                   / !
                  /  +-----------------------------------------------------------
```

X <variable>; Executes specified string.

In all these commands the n argument can be a constant like 12 or it can be "=<variable>;" where variable is the name of a variable. The semi-colon (;) is required when you use a variable in this way and you use the X command. Otherwise, a semi-colon is optional between commands.

Note: that values specified with the above commands will be reset to the system default when a BEEP sound is generated.

```
POKE <memory address>,<integer expression>
```

Example: POKE -31500,192
POKE &HF080,&HFF

Purpose: To write a byte into a memory location.

<memory address> is the address of the memory location to be POKEd. The <integer expression> is the data (byte) to be POKEd. It must be in the range 0 to 255.

<memory address> must be in the range -32768 to 65535. If this value is negative, address of the memory location is computed as subtracting from 65536. For example, -1 is the same as 65535 (65536-1). Otherwise, an Overflow error occurs.

```
PRESET <coordinate specifier>[,<colour>]
PSET <coordinate specifier>[,<colour>]
```

Example: PRESET (10,10),1
PSET STEP (100,50),12

Purpose: To set/reset the point at the specified coordinate and position the graphic cursor at the specified coordinate.

For the detail of the <coordinate specifier>, see the description of the PUT SPRITE statement.

The only difference between PSET and PRESET is that If no <colour> is given in the PRESET statement, the background colour is selected. When a <colour> argument is given, PRESET is identical to PSET.

```
PRINT [<list of expressions>]
```

Example: PRINT
PRINT "The answer is :";A + SIN(E)
PRINT A,SIN(A),COS(A),TAN(A)
PRINT TAB(30);"THE HEADING"

Purpose: To output data to the console.

If <list of expressions> is omitted, a blank line is printed. If <list of expressions> is included, the values of the expressions are printed at the console. An expression in the list may be a numeric and/or a string expression. Literal strings must be enclosed in quotation marks.

The position of each print item is determined by the punctuation used to separate the items in the list. Basic divides the line into print zones of 14 spaces each. In the <list of expressions>, a comma causes the next value to be printed as the beginning of the next zone. A semi-colon causes the next value to be printed immediately after the last value. Typing one or more spaces between expressions has the same effect as typing a semi-colon.

If a comma or a semi-colon terminates the <list of expressions>, the next PRINT statement begins printing on the same line, spacing accordingly. If the <list of expressions> terminates without a comma or semi-colon, a carriage return is printed at the end of the line. If the printed line is longer than the console width, Basic goes to the next physical line and continues printing.

Printed numbers are always followed by a space. Positive numbers are preceded by a space. Negative numbers are preceded by a minus sign (-). A question mark may be used in place of the word PRINT in a PRINT statement.

e.g. 'PRINT 6+7' is the same as '? 6+7'

Note: In MSX Basic PRINT will only output text in SCREEN 0 and SCREEN 1. (see PRINT #n).

```
PRINT USING <string expression>;<list of
expressions>
```

Example: PRINT USING "###.##";34.9
PRINT USING "THE @ OF JUNE";"5th"

Purpose: To print strings or numeric using a specified format.

<list of expressions> comprises the string expressions or numeric expressions that are to be printed separated by semi-colons.

<string expression> is a string literal (or variable) comprising special formatting characters. These formatting characters (see below) determine the field and the format of the printed strings or numbers.

When PRINT USING is used to print strings, one of three formatting characters may be used to format the string field:

"!"	Specified that only the first character in the given string is to be printed. A$ = "Tasmania" Ok PRINT USING "!";A$ T Ok
"&n spaces&"	Specified that 2+n characters from the string are to be printed. If the '&' signs are typed with no spaces, two characters will be printed; with one space three characters will be printed and so on. If the string is longer than the field, the extra characters are ignored. If the field is longer than the string, the string will be left-justified in the field and padded with spaces on the right. e.g. A$="Tasmania" Ok PRINT USING "& &";A$ Tas Ok
"@"	Specifies that the whole character in the given string is to be printed. e.g. A$="Tasmania" Ok PRINT USING "I love @ very much.";A$ I love Tasmania very much. Ok

When PRINT USING is used to print numbers, the following special characters may be used to format the numeric field:

"#" A number sign is used to represent each digit position. Digit positions are always filled. If the number to be printed has fewer digits than positions specified, the number will be right-justified (preceded by spaces) in the field.

"." A decimal point may be inserted at any position in the field. If the format string specifies that a digit is to precede the decimal point, the digit will always be printed (as 0 if necessary). Numbers are rounded as necessary.

e.g.

```
PRINT USING "###.##";10.5,4,6,4.888,.78
 10.50 4.00 6.00 4.89 0.78
Ok
```

"+" A plus sign at the beginning or end of the format string will cause the sign of the number (plus or minus) to be printed before or after the number.

e.g.

```
PRINT USING "+###.##";4.54,-4.54
 +5.54 -4.54
Ok
PRINT USING "###.##+";4.54,-4.54
4.54+ 4.54-
Ok
```

"-" A minus sign at the end of the format field will cause negative numbers to be printed with a trailing minus sign.

e.g.

```
PRINT USING "###.##-";4.54,-4.54
```

4.54 4.54-
Ok

"**" A double asterisk at the beginning of the format string causes leading spaces in the numeric field to be filled with asterisks. The ** also specifies positions for two or more digits.

e.g.

PRINT USING "**#.##";4.54,-4.54

**4.54 *-4.54

Ok

"$$" A double dollar sign causes a dollar sign to be printed to the immediate left of the formatted number. The $$ specifies two more digit positions, one of which is the dollar sign. The exponential format cannot be used with $$. Negative numbers cannot be used unless the minus sign trails to the right.

e.g.

PRINT USING "$$###.##";14.54,-14.54

$14.54 -$14.54

Ok

PRINT USING "$$###.##";14.54,-14.54

$14.54 $14.54-

Ok

"**$" The **$ at the beginning of a format string combines the effects of the above two symbols. Leading spaces will be asterisk-filled and a dollar sign will be printed before the number. **$ specifies three more digit positions, one of which is the dollar sign.

e.g.

PRINT USING "**$#.##";14.54

*$14.54
Ok

“,” A comma that is to the left of the decimal point in a formatting string causes a comma to be printed to the left of every third digit to the left of the decimal point. A comma that is at the end of the format string is printed as part of the string. A comma specifies another digit position. The comma has no effect if used with the exponential format.

e.g.

```
PRINT USING "####,.##";1145.4
 1,145.40
Ok

PRINT USING "####.##,";1145.4
 1145.40,
Ok
```

“^^^^” Four carats may be placed after the digit position characters to specify exponential format. The four carats allow space for E+xx to be printed. Any decimal point position may be specified. The significant digits are left-justified and the exponent is adjusted. Unless a leading + or trailing + or – is specified, one digit position will be used to the left of the decimal point to print a space or minus sign.

e.g.

```
PRINT USING "##.##^^^^";432.54
 4.32E+02
Ok

PRINT USING "#.##^^^^";-34.23
 3.423E+01-
Ok
```

PRINT USING "+#.##^^^^";43.21,-43.21
 +4.32E+01   -4.32E+01
Ok

"%"

If the number to be printed is larger than the specified numeric field, a percent sign is printed in front of the number. Also, if rounding causes the number to exceed the field, a percent sign will be printed in front of the rounded number.

e.g.

PRINT USING "##.##";432.11
 %432.11
Ok

PRINT USING ".##";.999
 %1.00
Ok

If the number of digits specified exceed 24 an Illegal function call error will result.

Note: In MSX Basic PRINT USING will only output text in SCREEN 0 and SCREEN 1. (see PRINT #n USING)

```
PUT (<exp1>,<exp2>),<arrayname>[,<operation>]
```

Example: PUT (50,50),A,XOR
PUT (100,10),V

Purpose: Output graphic pattern to screen after GET statement.

Output graphic patterns in the array to an assigned position on the screen, operation can be:

PSET Output pattern as is.

PRESET	Reverse pattern foreground/background colour.
AND	Combine graphic pattern colour with screen pattern.
OR	Graphic pattern overlapping the screen data.
XOR	Perform XOR with screen data. If the matching pixel from the array and the screen are the same then that pixel will be displayed in background colour else it will be displayed in the foreground colour.

```
PUT SPRITE <sprite plane number>[,<coordinate
specifier>][,<colour>][,<pattern number>]
```

Example: PUT SPRITE 1,(128,96),11,2
PUT SPRITE 1,STEP(10,10)

Purpose: To setup sprite attributes.

<sprite plane number> may range from 0 to 31.

<coordinates specifier> will always come in one of two forms:

(i) STEP (x offset, y offset) or
(ii) (absolute x, absolute y)

The first form is a point relative to the most recent point referenced. The second form is more common and directly refers to a point without regard to the last point referenced.

e.g. (10,10) absolute form
STEP(10,0) offset 10 in x and 0 in y
(0,0) origin (top left of screen)

Note that when Basic scans coordinate values it will allow them to be beyond the edge screen, however values outside the integer range (-32768 to 32767) will cause an overflow error. The values outside of the screen will be substituted with the nearest possible value. For example, 0 for any negative coordinate specification.

Note that (0,0) is always the upper left hand corner. It may seem strange to start numbering at the top so the bottom left corner is (0,191) in both high-resolution and medium resolution, but this is the standard.

The above description can be applied wherever graphic coordinates are used.

X coordinate <x> may range from -32 to 255. Y coordinates <y> may range from -32 to 191. If 208 (&HD0) is given to <y> all sprite planes behind disappear until a value other than 208 is given to that plane. If 209 (&HD1) is specified to <y> then the sprite disappears from the screen.

When a field is omitted, the current value is used. At start up, <colour> defaults to the current foreground colour.

<pattern number> specifies the pattern of sprite, and must be less than 256 when size of the sprite is 0 or 1 and must be less than 64 when size of the sprite is 2 or 3. <pattern number> defaults to the <sprite plane number>.

See also SCREEN statement and SPRITE$ variable.

RANDOMIZE

Note: This statement does not exist in SVI or MSX Basic

Purpose: To re-seed the Random Number Generator.

However the following will act as a re-seeder for the Random Number Generator.

e.g. N=RND(-TIME)

Note N is a dummy variable but may be used in later Random Number creation.

e.g. 5 N%=RND(-TIME)*99
10 PRINT RND(N%)

```
READ <list of variables>
```

Example: READ A,B,C,D
READ A$,G,D$(I),U$(7,9)

Purpose: To read values from a DATA statement and assign them to variables.

A READ statement must always be used in conjunction with a DATA statement. READ statements assign variables from DATA statement values on a one-to-one basis. READ statement variables may be numeric or string and the values read must agree with the variable types specified. If they do not agree, a Syntax error will result.

A single READ statement may access one or more DATA statements (they will be accessed in order), or several READ statements may access the same DATA statement. If the number of variables in <list of variables> exceeds the number of elements in the DATA statement(s), an Out of DATA error will result. If the number of variables specified is fewer than the number of elements in the DATA statement(s), subsequent READ statements will begin reading DATA at the first unread element. If there are no subsequent READ statements, the extra data is ignored.

To reread DATA statements from the start, use the RESTORE statement.

```
REM <remark>
```

Example: REM This is a remark statement.
' This is also a remark statement.

Purpose: To allow explanatory remarks to be inserted in a program.

REM statements are not executed but are shown exactly as entered when the program is LISTed.

REM statements may be branched into (from a GOTO or GOSUB statement) and execution will continue with the first executable statement after the REM statement.

REMarks may be added to the end of a line by preceding the REMark with a single quotation mark instead of REM.

e.g. PRINT 66*7 'total used.

Do not use this in a DATA statement as it would be considered legal data.

```
RESTORE [<line number>]
```

Example: RESTORE
RESTORE 500

Purpose: To allow DATA statements to be reread from a specified line.

After a RESTORE statement is executed, the next READ statement accesses the first item in the first DATA statement in the program. If <line number> is specified, the next READ statement access the first item in the specified DATA statement. If a non-existent line number is specified, an Undefined Line Number error will result.

```
RESUME [<operation>][<line number>]
```

Example: RESUME
RESUME 0
RESUME NEXT
RESUME 7000

Purpose: To continue program execution after an error recovery procedure has been performed.

Any one of the four formats shown above may be used, depending upon where execution is to resume.

RESUME or RESUME 0	Execution resumes at the statement which caused the error.
RESUME NEXT	Execution resumes at the statement immediately following the one which caused the error.
RESUME <line number>	Execution resumes at <line number>.

A RESUME statement that is not in an error trap subroutine causes a Resume without error error.

RETURN

Example: RETURN

Purpose: To return from a subroutine.

RETURN statement(s) in a subroutine cause Basic to branch back to the statement following the most recent GOSUB statement. A subroutine may contain more than one RETURN statement, should logic dictate a return at different points in the subroutine.

Subroutines may appear anywhere in the program, but it is recommended that the subroutine be readily distinguishable from the main program. To prevent inadvertent entry into the subroutine, it may be proceeded by a STOP, END or GOTO statement that directs the program control around the subroutine. Otherwise, a Return without Gosub error message is issued and execution is terminated.

```
SCREEN [<mode>][,<sprite size>][,<prompt line>]
(SVI Basic)
SCREEN [<mode>][,<sprite size>][,<key click
switch>][,<cassette baud rate>][,<printer
option>] (MSX Basic)
```

Example: SCREEN 1,2
SCREEN 0,0
SCREEN 0,0,0,1,0

Purpose: To assign the screen mode, <sprite size> and function key prompt line in SCREEN 0.

In SVI Basic <mode> should be set to 0 to select 40x24 text mode, 1 to select high resolution mode (256x192 graphics mode) and 2 to select multi colour (low-resolution mode).

In MSX Basic <mode> should be set to 0 to select 40x24 text mode, 1 to select 32z24 text mode, 2 to select high resolution mode (256x192 graphics mode) and 3 to select multi-colour (low-resolution mode).

<sprite size> determines the size of the sprites. Should be set to 0 to select 8x8 unmagnified sprites, 1 to select 8x8 magnified sprites, 2 to select 16x16 unmagnified sprites or 3 to select 16x16 magnified sprites. Note: If <sprite size> is specified, the contents of SPRITE$ will be cleared.

In SVI Basic <prompt line> will only work with SCREEN 0 and is used to turn on and off the bottom line of the text screen which displays the function key values. With a value of 1 to turn them n and 0 to turn them off.

In MSX Basic <key click switch> will turn the key click generated when you press a key on and off. With a value of 1 to turn it on and 0 to turn it off.

In MSX Basic <cassette baud rate> will select the rate at which programs will be saved to cassette, as a default. With of a value of 0 indication 1200 baud and a value of 1 indicating 2400 baud. Note: The baud rate can be changed using the CSAVE statement.

In MSX Basic <printer option> indicates whether you are using a printer that can print MSX graphics characters. A 0 selects an MSX printer and any other value selects a non-MSX printer.

```
SOUND <register of PSG>,<value to be written>
```

Example: SOUND 1,0
SOUND 6,15

Purpose: To write a value directly to the <register of PSG>.

	REGISTER	B7	B6	B5	B4	B3	B2	B1	B0
R0		8-bit Fine Tune A							
	Channel A Tone Period								
R1		XX	XX	XX	XX	4-bit Course Tune A			
R2		8-bit Fine Tune B							
	Channel B Tone Period								
R3		XX	XX	XX	XX	4-bit Course Tune B			
R4		8-bit Fine Tune c							
	Channel C Tone Period								
R5		XX	XX	XX	XX	4-bit Course Tune C			
R6	Noise Period	XX	XX	XX	5-bit Period Control				
					Noise			Tone	
R7	Noise Mixer	ioB	ioA	C	B	A	C	B	A
R8	Channel A Amplitude	XX	XX	XX	M	L3	L2	L1	L0
R9	Channel B Amplitude	XX	XX	XX	M	L3	L2	L1	L0
R10	Channel C Amplitude	XX	XX	XX	M	L3	L2	L1	L0
R11		8-bit Fine Tune E							
	Envelope Period								
R12		8-bit Course Tune E							
R13	Envelope	XX	XX	XX	XX	Cont	Att	Alt	Hold

	Shape/Cycle								
R14	I/O Port A Data Store	8-bit Parallel I/O on Port A							
R15	I/O Port B Data Store	8-bit Parallel I/O on Port B							

SOUND [ON/OFF] (SVI Basic Only)

Example: SOUND ON
SOUND OFF

Purpose: To send audio output from the cassette recorder to the Television speaker.

Early Spectravideo Data Cassette recorders had the facility to record a voice track along side of the Program recorded on a data cassette. The SOUND ON/OFF statement allows the user to turn on or off this sound track while loading programs. This recording option is no longer available on Data Cassettes but the SOUND on/off statement should still work with cassettes recorded on earlier equipment.

SPRITE [ON/OFF/STOP]

Example: SPRITE ON
SPRITE STOP

Purpose: To activate/deactivate trapping of sprites in a Basic program.

A SPRITE ON statement must be executed to activate trapping of sprites. After a SPRITE ON statement, if a line number is specified in the ON SPRITE GOSUB statement then every time Basic starts a new statement it will check to see if the sprites coincide. If so it will perform a GOSUB to the line number specified in the ON SPRITE GOSUB statement.

If a SPRITE OFF statement has been executed, no trapping takes place and the event is not remembered even if it does take place.

If a SPRITE STOP statement has been executed, no trapping will take place, but if the sprites coincide this is remembered so an immediate trap will take place when SPRITE ON is executed.

STOP

Example: STOP

Purpose: To terminated program execution and return to command level.

STOP statements may be used anywhere in a program to terminate execution. When a STOP statement is encountered, the following message is printed:

Break in nnnn (nnnn is a line number)

Unlike the END statement, the STOP statement does not close files.

Execution is resumed by issuing a CONT command.

STOP [ON/OF/STOP]

Example: STOP ON
STOP STOP

Purpose: To activate/deactivate trapping of a Control-STOP.

A STOP ON statement must be executed to activate trapping of a Control-STOP. After a STOP ON statement, if a line number is specified in the ON STOP GOSUB then every time Basic starts a new statement it will check to see if a Control-STOP was pressed. If so, it will perform a GOSUB to the line number specified in the ON STOP GOSUB statement.

If a STOP OFF statement has been executed, no trapping takes place and the event is not remembered even if it does take place.

If a STOP STOP statement has been executed, no trapping will take place, but if a control-STOP is pressed this is remembered so an immediate trap will take place when STOP ON is executed.

STRIG (<n>) [ON/OFF/STOP]

Example: STRIG (0) ON
STRIG (4) OFF

Purpose: To activate/deactivate trapping of the trigger buttons of the joysticks in a Basic program.

<n> can be in the range 0 to 4. If <n>=0, the space bar is used for a trigger button. If <n> is either 1 or 3, the trigger of a joystick in port 1 is used. If <n> is either 2 or 4, the trigger of a joystick in port 2 is used.

A STRIG(n) ON statement must be executed to activate trapping of a trigger button. After a STRIG(n) ON statement, if a line number is specified in the ON STRIG GOSUB statement then every time Basic starts a new statement it will check to see if the trigger button was pressed. If so it will perform a GOSUB to the line number specified in the ON STRIG GOSUB statement.

If a STRIG(n) OFF statement has been executed, no trapping takes place and the event is not remembered even if it does take place.

If a STRIG(n) STOP statement has been executed, no trapping will take place, but if the trigger button is pressed this is remembered so an immediate trap will take place when STRIG(n) ON is executed.

SWAP <variable>,<variable>

Example: SWAP A,M(I)
SWAP A$,M$

Purpose: To exchange the value of two variables.

Any type of variable may be SWAPed (integer, single precision, double precision or sting), but the two variables must be of the same type or a Type mismatch error results.

SWITCH (SVI Basic only)

Example: SWITCH

Purpose: Function to switch between memory banks. Note: This command only works if you have a 64k RAM expansion cartridge installed.

If you have a 64K RAM expansion card installed in your SVI-318/328 you can store a different BASIC program in each bank. (The normal memory and the expansion cartridge).

The SWITCH command changes from one bank to another.

VDP(<n>) = <m> (MSX Basic only)

Example: VDP(1)=10
N = VDP(2)

Purpose: To write and read from the Video Display Processor's VDP registers.

<n> can be from 0 to 7 and <m> be from 0 to 255.

VPOKE <address in VRAM>,<value to be written>

Example: VPOKE 4000,18
VPOKE &H500,&HFF

Purpose: To poke a value to a specified location in VRAM.

<address in VRAM> can be in the range 0 to 16383.

<value to be written> should be a byte value (0 to 255).

WAIT <port number>,I[J]

Example: WAIT &H34,0
WAIT 52,0,&H0C

Purpose: To suspend program execution while monitoring the status of a machine input port.

The WAIT statement causes execution to be suspended until a specified machine input port develops a specified bit pattern. The data read at the port is exclusive OR'ed with the integer expression J and then AND'ed with the integer expression I.

If the result is zero, Basic loops back and reads the data at the port again. If the result is non-zero, execution continues with the next statement. If J is omitted, it is assumed to be zero.

Disk Commands and Functions

The following section is only of interest if you have one or two disk drives. This section contains both STATEMENTS and FUNCTIONS used by Basic to access the Disk.

ATTR$(<drive:> <#filenumber> <filename>) (SVI Basic only)

Example: PRINT ATTR$(#1)
A$ = ATTR$("2:TEST")

Purpose: To return disk attributes.

ATTR$ returns a string of the current attributes for a drive, currently open file or file that need not be open.

Also see the SET command for File attributes.

CLOSE [[#]<file number>[,<file number>]]

Example: CLOSE
CLOSE 1,4

Purpose: To close the channel and releases the buffer associated with it.

If no <file number>s are specified, all open channels are closed.

COPY <drive> FROM <drive>/<file> (SVI Basic only)
COPY <file specifier> TO <file specifier> (MSX Basic only)

Example: COPY 1 FROM 2 (SVI)
COPY 1 FROM "2:FRED" (SVI)
COPY "A:FRED.BAS" TO "B:" (MSX)
COPY "A:FRED" TO "B:JOHN" (MSX)

Purpose: To copy files from one disk to another.

In SVI Basic the COPY command can only be used with dual disk systems. In MSX Basic with a single disk drive Basic pretends that the computer has two drives and asks you to swap disks.

You may COPY entire disks by only specifying drive numbers or you may COPY single files by name.

Note: COPYing to and from cassette gives unusual results and should be avoided.

CVI(<2-byte string>)
CVS(<4-byte string>)
CVD(<8-byte string)

Example: F=CVS(N$)
PRINT CVI("44")+8

Purpose: To convert string values to numeric values.

Numeric values that are read from a random disk file must be converted from strings back into numbers.

- CVI converts 2-byte strings to an integer.
- CVS converts 4-byte strings to single precision numbers.
- CVD converts 8-byte strings to double precision numbers.

See also MKI$, MKS$ and MKD$.

DSKF(<drive number>)

Example: PRINT DSKF(1)
A = DSKF(2)

Purpose: To show how much space is left on a disk.

For SVI Basic the number returned by DSKF is in blocks, that is 4K sections of a disk. If the reply to PRINT DSKF(1) is 2 then that disk has 8K of free space left before it is full. The maximum free space on a SVI Basic blank disk is 144k or 36 blocks.

For MSX Basic the number returned by DSKF is the number of kilobytes left. The maximum free space on an MSX disk is 360k (or 720k depending on your drive type).

```
DSKI$(<drive>,<track>,<sector>) (SVI Basic only)
DSKI$(<drive number>,<logical sector>) (MSX
Basic only)
```

Example: A$=DSKI$(1,I,J) (SVI)
PRINT DSKI$(2,0,12) (SVI)
A$=DSKI$(1,I) (MSX)
PRINT DSKI$(2,12) (MSX)

Purpose: To read a string from a specified sector.

DSKI$ returns the contents of a sector to a string variable name.

```
DSKO$(<drive>,<track>,<sector>,<string
expression>) (SVI Basic only)
DSKO$(<drive number>,<logical sector>,<string
expression>) (MSX Basic only)
```

Example: DSKO$(1,0,12,Z$) (SVI)
DSKO$(2,1,5,T$) (SVI)
DSKO$(1,12,Z$) (MSX)
DSKO$(2,24,Z$) (MSX)

Purpose: To write a string onto the specified sector.

The maximum length for the string is 128 characters. A string of fewer than 128 characters is zero filled at the end to 128 characters.

```
EOF(<file number>)
```

Example: IF EOF(1) GOTO 5
A = EOF(4)

Purpose: To test for end-of-file.

Returns -1 (true) if the end of a sequential file has been reached. Use EOF to test for end-of-file while INPUTing, to avoid Input past end errors.

```
FIELD [#]<file number>,<field width> AS <string variable>...
```

Example:	FIELD #1,30 AS Z$ FIELD #2,20 AS A$, 10 AS F$, 40 AS R$
Purpose:	To allocate space for variables in a random file buffer.

To get data out of a random buffer after a GET or to enter data before a PUT, a FIELD statement must have been executed.

<file number> is the number under which the file was OPENed.

<field with> is the number of characters to be allocated to <string variable>.

FIELD does NOT place any data in the random file buffer. (See LSET/RSET and GET)

The total number of bytes allocated in a FIELD statement must not exceed the record length that was specified when the file was OPENed. Otherwise, a Field overflow error occurs. The default record length is 128.

Any number of FIELD statements may be executed for the same file and all FIELD statements that have been executed are in effect at the same time.

Note: Do not use FIELDed variable names in an INPUT or LET statement. Once a variable name is FIELDed, it points to the correct place in the random file buffer. If a subsequent INPUT or LET statement with that variable name is executed, the variable's pointer is moved to string space.

```
[L]FILES <drive number> (SVI Basic only)
[L]FILES [<file specifier>] (MSX Basic only)
```

Example: FILES 2 (SVI)
LFILES
FILES "A:*.BAS" (MSX)
FILES "ABC.???" (MSX)

Purpose: To display the FILES on a disk.

<file specifier> can be any valid drive letter and file name. The wild cards * and ? can be used to display files in groups.

FILES displays to the terminal.

LFILES prints to the printer.

```
FPOS(<file number>)
```

Example: A = FPOS(1)
PRINT FPOS(3)

Purpose: To display the position of a disk file.

FPOS is the same as the LOC function except it returns the number of the physical sector when <file number> is located.

```
GET [#]<file number>[,<record number>]
```

Example: GET #1,I
GET #2,6

Purpose: To read a record from a random disk file into the random access buffer.

If the "buffer changed" flag is set, write the buffer to disk. Then execute the GET (read the record into the buffer), and reset the position for sequential I/O to the beginning of the buffer.

`INPUT #<file number>,<variable list>`

Example: INPUT #1,A
INPUT #2,A$,S,G(I)

Purpose: To read data items from the specified channel and assign them to program variables.

The type of data in the file must match the type specified by the <variable list>. Unlike the INPUT statement, no question mark is printed with the INPUT# statement.

The data items in the file should appear just as they would if data were being typed in response to an INPUT statement. With numeric values, leading spaces, carriage returns and line feeds are ignored. The first character encountered that is not a space, carriage return or line feed is assumed to be the start of a number. The number terminates on a space, carriage return, line feed or comma.

Also, if Basic is scanning the data for a string item, leading spaces, carriage returns and line feeds are ignored. The first character encountered that is not a space, carriage return or line feed is assumed to be the start of a string item. If this first character is a double-quotation mark ("), the string item will consist of all characters read between the first quotation mark and the second. Thus a quoted string may not contain a quotation mark as a character.

If the first character of the string is not a quotation mark, the string is an unquoted string and will terminate on a comma, carriage return, line feed or after 255 characters have been read. If end-of-file is reached when a numeric or string item in being INPUTed, the item is terminate.

`LINE INPUT #<file number>,<string variable>`

Example: LINE INPUT #1,A$

Purpose: To read an entire line (up to 254 characters), without delimiters, from a sequential file to a string variable.

<file number> is the number which the file was OPENed to.

<string variable> is the name of the string variable to which the line will be assigned.

LINE INPUT # reads all characters in the sequential file up to a carriage return. It then skips over the carriage return/line feed sequence and the next LINE INPUT # reads all characters up to the next carriage return. (If a line feed/carriage return sequence is encountered it is preserved. That is, the line feed/carriage return characters are returned as part of the string).

LINE INPUT # is especially useful if each line of a file has been broken into fields, or if a Spectravideo Basic program saved in ASCII mode is being read as data by another program.

```
INPUT$(n[#}<file number>)
```

Example: A$ = INPUT$(5,#1)
PRINT INPUT$(30,2)

Purpose: To return a string of n characters, read from the file.

<file number> is the number which the file was OPENed to.

```
IPL ["<command> …] (SVI Basic only)
```

Example: IPL "FILES"
IPL "SCREEN,0:FILES"

Purpose: To load a command onto a disk that will performed on a cold boot.

IPL (initial Program Load) is used to customize a disk.

e.g. IPL "RUN"+CHR$(34)+"1:MENU"

This IPL command will allow MENU to automatically run every time the Spectravideo Computer is turned on with that disk in the first drive.

KILL "<drive number>:<file number>" (SVI Basic only)
KILL "[<drive identifier>]<file name>" (MSX Basic only)

Example: KILL "1:FRED" (SVI)
KILL "1:MENU.ONE" (SVI)
KILL "A:FRED" (MSX)
KILL "B:MENU.ONE" (MSX)

Purpose: To delete a file from disk.

If a KILL statement is given for a file that is currently OPEN, a File already open error occurs.

KILL is used for all types of disk files.

LOC(<file number>)

Example: IF LOC(1)>50 THEN STOP
PRINT LOC(2)

Purpose: To return file information.

With random disk files, LOC returns the next record number to be used if a GET or PUT (without a record number) is executed.

With sequential files, LOC returns the number of sectors (128 byte blocks) read from or written to the file since it was OPENed.

LOF(<file number>)

Example: IF NUM>LOF(1) THEN PRINT"INVALID"
A = LOF(4)

Purpose: Returns the number of records present in the last extent read or written.

If the file does not exceed one extent (125 records), then OF returns the true length of the file.

```
LSET <string variable> = <string expression>
RSET <string variable> = <string expression>
```

Example: LSET A$ = MKS$(A)
LSET D$ = D1$
RSET A$ = N$

Purpose: To move data from memory to a random file buffer (in preparation for a PUT statement).

If <string expression> requires fewer bytes than were FIELDed to <string variable> LSET left justifies the string in the field, and RSET right justifies the string. Spaces are used to pad the extra positions. If the string is too long for the field, characters are dropped from the right. Numeric values must be converted to strings before they are LSET or RSET.

LSET or RSET may also be used with non-fielded string variables to left justify or right justify a string in a given field. This can be very handy for formatted printed output.

```
MAXFILES=<number of files>
```

Example: MAXFILES=3
MAXFILES=8

Purpose: To set aside buffer space for file handling.

When using files, MAXFILES must be used when more than one file is to be OPENed.

```
MKI$(<integer expression>)
MKS$(<single precision expression>)
MKD$(<double precision expression>)
```

Example: D$ = MKS$(A)
G$ = MKI$(6)

Purpose: To convert numeric values to string values.

Any numeric value that is placed in a random file buffer with LSET or RSET statements must be converted to a string.

- MKI$ converts an integer to a 2-byte string.
- MKS$ converts a single precision number to a 4-byte string.
- MKD$ converts a double precision number to a 8-byte string.

```
NAME <drive spec> <old filename> AS <drive spec>
<new filename>
```

Example: NAME "1:FRED" AS "1:SAM" (SVI)
NAME "2:TEST.ONE" AS "2:TEST.BAK" (SVI)
NAME "A:FRED" AS "A:SAM" (MSX)

Purpose: To change the name of a disk file.

<old filename> must exist and <new filename> must not exist; otherwise an error will result.

After a NAME command, the file exists on the same disk, in the same area of disk space, with the new name.

```
OPEN <filename> [FOR <mode>] AS [#]<file number>
[LEN=<n>] (SVI Basic only)
OPEN <filename> [FOR <mode>] AS [#]<file number>
[LEN=<n>] (MSX Basic only)
```

Example: OPEN "1:FRED" AS #1 (SVI)
OPEN "2:TEXT.TMP" FOR OUTPUT AS #1 (SVI)
OPEN "A:FRED" AS #1 (MSX)

Purpose: To allow I/O to a disk file.

<mode> is one of the following:

INPUT, OUTPUT, APPEND

If [FOR <mode>] is not specified the file is assumed to be Random access.

The mode determines only the initial positioning within the file an the actions to be taken if the file does not exist.

The action taken in each mode is:

INPUT:	The initial position is at the start of the file. An error is returned if the file is not found.
OUTPUT:	The initial position is at the start of the file. A new file is always created.
APPEND:	The initial position is at the end of the file. An error is returned if the file is not found.
	If the FOR <mode> is omitted, the initial position is at the start of the file. If the file is not found, it is created.

Note: Variable length records are not supported in Spectravideo Basic. All records are 128 bytes in length.

At any one time, it is possible to have a particular filename OPEN under more than one file number. This allows different attributes to be used for different purposes. Or, for program clarity, you may wish to use different file numbers for different methods of access. Each file number has a different buffer, so changes made under one file are not accessible to (or affected by) the other numbers until that record is written (e.g. GET #n,LOC(n)).

When a file is OPENed FOR APPEND, the file mode is set to APPEND and the record number is set to the last record of the file. The program may subsequently execute disk I/O statements that move the pointer elsewhere in the file. When the last record is read, the file mode is reset to FILE and the pointer is left at the end of the file. Then, if you wish to APPEND another record execute:

GET #n,LOF(n)

In MSX Basic the length of the records can be changed from the standard 128 bytes to the value specified in <n>.

e.g. LEN = 32

```
PRINT#<file number>,<exp>
PRINT#<file number>,USING <string
expression>;<list of expressions>
```

Example: PRINT #1,A$
PRINT #1,USING "###.##";55.8

Purpose: To write data items to the specified channel.

See PRINT, PRINT USING statements for details.

```
PUT[#]<file number>[,<record number>]
```

Example: PUT #1,D%
PUT #2

Purpose: To write a record from a random buffer to a random disk file.

<file number> is the number under which the file was OPENed. If <record number> is omitted, the record will have the next available record number (after the last PUT). The largest possible record number is 32767.

```
SET <drive>[#file]<filename>,<attribute string>
(SVI Basic Only)
```

Example: SET 1,"R"
SET "1:FRED","P"

Purpose: To set File and drive attributes.

The SET statement determines the attributes of the currently mounted disk, a currently open file or a file that need not be open.

<attribute string> is a string of characters that determines what attributes are set. Any character other than the following are ignored:

R	Read after Write
P	Write Protect

External Device Channels

In the previous section disk commands were explained, however some of these commands may also be used with other devices in the same manner as with the disk.

These commands are:

- CLOSE
- INPUT#
- INPUT$
- LINE INPUT#
- OPEN
- PRINT#
- PRINT # USING

For details of these commands see the previous sections.

They be used on the following devices:

Device	SVI Name	MSX Name	Type
Keyboard	KYBD	N/A	Input
Printer	LPT	LPT	Output
Graphics	N/A	GRP	Output
Screen	CRT	CRT	Output
Disk 1	1	A	Input/Output
Disk 2	2	B	Input/Output
Cassette	CAS	CAS	Input/Output
Modem	MOD	COM	Input/Output

You may only use sequential files.

e.g.

```
10 MAXFILES=2
20 OPEN "LPT:FRED" FOR OUTPUT AS #1
30 OPEN "CAS:FREDI" FOR INPUT AS #2
40 IF EOF(2) GOTO 80
50 INPUT #2,A$
60 PRINT #1,A$
70 GOTO 40
```

```
80 CLOSE
90 END
```

In the above sample program data is read from the Cassette Record and printed to the Printer.

Intrinsic Functions

The intrinsic functions provided by Basic are presented in this section. The functions may be called from any program without further definition.

ABS(X)

Example: PRINT ABS(7*(-5))

Purpose: Returns the absolute value of the expression X.

ASC(X$)

Example: PRINT ASC("PETER")

Purpose: Returns a numeric value that is the ASCII code of the first character of the string X$. If X$ is null, an Illegal function call error is returned.

ATN(X)

Example: PRINT ATN(3)

Purpose: Returns the arctangent of X in radians. Result is in the range –pi/2 to pi/2. The expression X may be any numeric type, but evaluation of ATN is always performed in double precision.

BASE(<n>) (MSX Basic only)

Example: PRINT BASE(0)
0

Purpose: Gives the current base address position of the various screen tables in the video RAM.

The value of <n> determines which table to return as follows:

0 base address of name table in text mode 0
1 unused

2 base address of pattern generator in text mode 0
3 unused
4 unused
5 base address of name table in text mode 1
6 base address of colour table in text mode 1
7 base address of pattern generator in text mode 1
8 base address of sprite attribute table in text mode 1
9 base address of sprite pattern table in text mode 1
10 base address of name table in high resolution mode 2
11 base address of colour table in high resolution mode 2
12 base address of pattern generator in high resolution mode 2
13 base address of sprite attribute table in high resolution mode 2
14 base address of sprite pattern table in high resolution mode 2
15 base address of name table in multi-colour graphics mode 3
16 unused
17 base address of pattern table in multi-colour graphics mode 3
18 base address of sprite attribute table in multi-colour graphics mode 3
19 base address of sprite pattern table in multi-colour graphics mode 3

`BIN$(X)`

Example: PRINT BIN$(5)

Purpose: Returns a string representing the binary value of the decimal argument. X is a numeric expression in the range -32765 t 65535. If X is negative, the two's complement of it is used. That is BIN$(-X) is the same as BIN$(65536-X).

`CDBL(X)`

Example: PRINT CDBL(A)

Purpose: Converts X to a double precision number.

CHR$(I)

Example: PRINT CHR$(66)

Purpose: Returns a string whose one element has ASCII code I. CHR$ is commonly used to send a special character to the terminal. For instance, the ESC character could be sent (CHR$(27)) as a preface to a terminal code.

CINT(X)

Example: PRINT CINT(54.76)

Purpose: Converts X to an integer by round the fractional portion. If X is not in the range -32768 to 32767, an Overflow error occurs. See also CDBL, CSNG, FIX and INT.

COS(X)

Example: PRINT 3*COS(.5)

Purpose: Returns the cosine of X in radians. The calculation of COS(X) is performed in double precision.

CSNG(X)

Example: PRINT CSNG(A#)

Purpose: Converts X to a single precision number. See also CINT and CDBL.

CSRLIN

Example: PRINT CSRLIN

Purpose: Returns the vertical coordinate of the cursor.

ERR/ERL

Example: IF ERR=23 THEN PRINT"WRONG"
IF ERL<1000 GOTO 50

Purpose: When an error handling subroutine is entered, the variable ERR contains the error code for error. The variable ERL contains the line number in which the error was detected. Because ERL and ERR are reserved variables, neither may appear to the left of the equal sign in a LET statement.

EXP(X)

Example: PRINT EXP(X-1)

Purpose: Returns e to the power of X. X must be <= 145.06286085862. If EXP overflows, the Overflow error message is printed.

FIX(X)

Example: PRINT FIX(8.7)

Purpose: Returns the integer part of X. FIX(X) is equivalent to SGN(X)*INT(ABS(X)). The major different between FIX and INT is that FIX does not return the next lower number for negative X.

FRE(0)
FRE("")

Example: PRINT FRE(0),FRE("")

Purpose: Arguments to FRE are dummy arguments. FRE returns the number of bytes in memory not being used by Basic. FRE(0) returns the number of bytes in memory which can be used for Basic programs.

FRE("") returns the number of bytes in memory for string space.

HEX$(X)

Example: A$ = HEX$(45)

Purpose: Returns a string which represents the hexadecimal value of the decimal argument.

INKEY$

Example: IF INKEY$="" GOTO 10

Purpose: Returns either a one-character string containing a character read from the keyboard or a null string if no key is pressed. No characters will be echoed and all characters are passed through to the program except Control-STOP, which terminates the program.

INPUT$(X)

Example: A$ = INPUT$(8)

Purpose: Returns a string of X characters, read from the keyboard. No characters will be echoed and all characters are passed except Control-STOP, which terminates the program.

INP(I)

Example: A = INP(255)

Purpose: Returns the byte read from port I. I must be in the rand 1 to 255. INP is the complementary function to the OUT statement.

INSTR([I,]X$,Y$)

Example: B = INSTR("TASMANIA","MAN")

Purpose: Searches for the first occurrence of string Y$ in X$ and returns the position at which the match is found. Option offset I, sets the position for starting the search. If must be in the range 0 to 255. If I>LEN(X$) or if X$ is null or Y$ cannot be found or X$ and Y$ are null, INSTR returns 0. If only Y$ is null, INSTR returns I or 1. X$ and Y$ may be string variables, string expressions or string literals.

`INT(X)`

Example: PRINT INT(9,6)

Purpose: Returns the largest integer <=X.

`LEFT$(X$,I)`

Example: PRINT LEFT$("HOLIDAY",4)

Purpose: Returns a string comprising the leftmost I characters of X$, I must be in the range 0 to 255. If I is greater than LEN(X$), the entire string (X$) is returned. IF I=0 a null string is returned.

`LEN(X$)`

Example: PRINT LEN(D$)

Purpose: Returns the number of characters in X$. Nonprinting characters and blanks are counted.

`LOG(X)`

Example: A = LOG(6)

Purpose: Returns the natural logarithm of X. X must be greater than zero.

`LPOS(X)`

Example: A = LPOS(X)

Purpose: Returns the current position of the printer print head within the printer buffer. It does not necessarily give the physical location of the print head. X is a dummy argument.

`MID$(X$,I[,J])`

Example: PRINT MID$("TUESDAY",2,3)

Purpose: Returns a string of length J characters from X$ beginning with the Ith character. I and J must be in the range 1 to 255. If J is omitted or if there are fewer than J characters, al rightmost characters beginning with the Ith character are returned. If I>LEN(X$), MID$ returns a null string.

`OCT$(N)`

Example: PRINT OCT$(30)

Purpose: Returns a string which represents the octal value of the decimal argument. N is a numeric expression in the range -32766 to 65535. If N is negative, the two's compliment of it is used. That is, OCT$(-N) is the same as OCT$(65536-N).

`PAD(N)`

Example: PRINT PAD(2)

Purpose: Returns various status of the touch pad.

N can be in the range 0 to 7.

When 0 to 3 is specified, the touch pad connected to joystick port 1 is selected, when 4 to 7 port 2 is used.

When N = 0 or 4 the status of the touch pad is returned, -1 when touched, 0 when released.

When N = 1 or 5, the X coordinate is returned.

When N = 2 or 6, the Y coordinate is returned.

When N = 3 or 7, the status of the switch on the pad is returned, -1 when pushed, 0 otherwise.

`PDL(N)`

Example: PRINT PDL(1)

Purpose: Returns the value of a paddle.

N can be in the range 1 to 12.

When N is either 1,3,5,7,9 or 11 the paddle connected to port 1 is used.

When N is either 2,4,6,8,10 or 12 the paddle connected to port 2 is used.

`PEEK(I)`

Example: A = PEEK(32767)

Purpose: Returns the byte (decimal integer in the range 0 to 255) read from memory location I. I must be in the range -32767 to 65535. PEEK is the complimentary function to the POKE statement.

`POINT(X,Y)`

Example: A = POINT(10,100)

Purpose: Returns the colour of a specified pixel.

`POS(I)`

Example: A = POS(0)

Purpose: Returns the current cursor position. The left most position is 0. I is a dummy argument.

`RIGHT$(X$,I)`

Example: PRINT RIGHT$("HELLO",2)

Purpose: Returns the rightmost I characters of string X$. If I=LEN(X$), X$ is returned. If I=0 a null string is returned.

`RND(X)`

Example: PRINT RND(1)*8

Purpose: Returns a random number between 0 and 1. The same sequence of numbers is generated each time a program is RUN. If X < 0, the random generator is reseeded for any given X. X = 0 repeats the last number generated. X >0 generates the next random number in the sequence.

`SGN(X)`

Example: PRINT SGN(3)

Purpose: Returns 1 for X > 0, 0 for X = 0 and -1 for X < 0.

`SIN(X)`

Example: PRINT SIN(A)

Purpose: Returns the sine of X in radians. SIN(X) is calculated in double precision.

`SPACE$(X)`

Example: PRINT "ONE";SPACE$(5);"TWO"

Purpose: Returns a string of spaces of length X. The expression X discards the fractional portion and must be in the range 0 to 255.

SPC(I)

Example: PRINT SPC(25);

Purpose: Prints I blanks on the screen. SPC may only be used with PRINT and LPRINT statements. I must be in the range 0 to 255.

SPRITE$(X)

Example: SPRITE$(1)=A$

Purpose: To create the patterns of sprites.

X must be less than 256 when the size of sprites is 0 or 1, less than 64 when the size of sprites is 2 or 3.

The length of this variable is fixed to 32 bytes, so, if assigning a string that is shorter than 32 characters, CHR$(0) are added to the end.

SQR(X)

Example: PRINT SQR(66)

Purpose: Returns the square root of X. X mist be >=0.

STICK(X)

Example: A = STICK(0)

Purpose: Returns the direction of a joystick. X can be in the range of 0 to 2. If X = 0, the cursor keys are used as a joystick. If X is either 1 or 2, the joystick connected to port 1 or 2 is used.

STRIG(X)

Example: A = STRIG(1)

Purpose: Returns the status of a trigger button of a joystick. X can be in the range of 0 to 4.

If X = 0, the space bar is used for the trigger button.

If X is either 1 or 3, the first or second triggers of the joystick in port one is used.

If X is either 2 or 4, the first or second triggers of the joystick in port two is used.

0 is returned if a trigger is not being pressed, -1 is returned overwise.

`STR$(X)`

Example: A$ = STR$(8)

Purpose: Returns the string representation of the value of X.

`STRING$(I,J)`
`STRING$(I,X$)`

Example: PRINT STRING$(6,"*")

Purpose: Returns a string of length I whose characters all have the ASCII code J or the first character of the string X$.

`TAB(I)`

Example: PRINT TAB(44);"HELLO"

Purpose: Spaces to position I on the console.

If the current print position is already beyond space I, TAB does nothing.

Space 0 is the leftmost position and the rightmost position is the width minus one.

I must be in the range 0 to 255.

TAB may only be used with PRINT and LPRINT statements.

`TAN(X)`

Example: PRINT TAN(3)

Purpose: Return the tangent of X in radians. TAN(X) is calculated to double precision. If TAN overflows, an Overflow error will occur.

`TIME`

Example: PRINT TIME
TIME = 0

Purpose: To store the passing of time in intervals of TIME/50 seconds (TIME/60 for NTSC machines).

TIME is set like any variable with a LET statement.

TIME will still increment when in EDIT mode.

`USR[<digit>](X)`

Example: A = USR4(88)

Purpose: Calls the user's assembly language subroutine with the argument X.

<digit> is in the range 0 to 9 and corresponds to the digit supplied with the DEFUSR statement for the routine.

If <digit> is omitted, USR0 is assumed.

`VARPTR(<variable name>)`
`VARPTR(#<file number>)`

Example: A = VARPTR(A(5))
S = VARPTR(#1)

Purpose: Returns the address of the first byte of data identified with <variable name>.

A value must be assigned to <variable name> prior to the execution of VARPTR, otherwise an Illegal function call error results.

Any type variable name can be used (numeric, string, array), and the address returned will be an integer in the range -32768 to 32767.

If a negative address is returned, add it to 65536 to obtain the actual address.

```
VPEEK(<address in VRAM>)
```

Example: R = VPEEK(456)

Purpose: Returns a value of VRAM specified. <address in VRAM> can be in the range of 0 to 16383.

Appendix A – Error Codes

Code		Message	Meaning
SVI	MSX		
1	1	Next without For	A NEXT command has been found before a matching FOR command.
2	2	Syntax error	Cannot understand the command.
3	3	Return without Gosub	A RETURN was encountered before a GOSUB command.
4	4	Out of Data	Too many read statements for the amount of data supplied.
5	5	Illegal function call	Cannot perform the command. Requires further information.
6	6	Overflow	Result of calculations exceeds allowable value or memory location greater than 65535.
7	7	Out of memory	Insufficient memory space for the function required.
8	8	Undefined line number	An attempt was made to GOTO or GOSUB to a non-existent line number.
9	9	Subscript out of range	The subscripted variable exceeds the array size when A$ was DIM'd.
10	10	Redimensioned array	Attempt to change the size of an array without ERASEing it.
11	11	Division by zero	An attempt was made to divide by zero.
12	12	Illegal direct	Use of INPUT as a direct command.
13	13	Type mismatch	Trying to perform string manipulation on a numeric variable and vice versa.
14	14	Out of string space	Insufficient string space was CLEARed for string function.
15	15	String too long	String length exceeds 255 characters.
16	16	String formula too complex	BASIC can't work out what you mean.
17	17	Can't continue	Can't CONTinue after a STOP or BREAK encountered.
18	18	Undefined user functions	Tried to execute a USER call before a DEFUSR statement for that routine.
19	19	Device I/O error	Interrupt to an input or output function e.g. saving to tape or disk.
20	20	Verify error	Error while using the CLOAD? i.e. when verifying that a program was CSAVEd correctly.

Code		Message	Meaning
SVI	MSX		
21	21	No resume	The end of the program has been reached in error trapping mode.
22	22	Resume without error	RESUME was encountered before executing an ON ERROR GOTO
23	23	Unprintable error	Attempt to simulate an ERROR with an invalid id code.
24	24	Missing operand	Information given is incomplete.
25	5	Line buffer overflow low	Line entered is too long.
26-49	26-49	Unprintable error	Future expansion.
50	50	Field overflow	A random-access buffer was allocated more than 255 bytes.
51	51	Internal error	Disk I/O fault or, error in disk operating system.
52	52	Bad file number	File buffer number has not been assigned to a file using an OPEN statement.
53	53	File not found	File named is not on the disk. Check file name and extension.
54	54	File already open	Attempt to open a file that has not been closed.
55	55	Input past end	INPUT statement encountered after all information was read from a sequential file.
56	56	Bad file name	Name given to file was not in the correct format.
57	57	Direct statement in file	Attempt to LOAD, RUN or MERGE a non-BASIC file.
58 	 58	Sequence after put Sequence I/O only	Using PUT or GET on a file which is not random access.
60	59	File not open	Attempt to get input from closed file.
61	60	Bad allocation table	Allocation table on disk does not match the one in memory.
	61	Bad file mode	Incorrect use f INPUT and OUTPUT with the OPEN command.
62	62	Bad drive number/name	
63	63	Bad track/sector	Track/sector number if incorrect.
64	64	File still open	Attempt to OPEN a file which has not been closed.

Code		Message	Meaning
SVI	MSX		
65		Disk not mounted	The disk is not in the drive.
66		Deleted record	
67	5	File already exists	
68	66	Disk full	
	67	Too many files	Too many entries in directory
	68	Disk write protected	
69		File write protected	Attempting to write to a file which is write protected.
70	69	Disk error	Error occurred while accessing a disk.
71	70	Disk offline	Disk not in drive.
72	71	Rename across disk	RENAME command cannot be used from one disk to another.

Appendix B I/O Port Locations

Spectravideo 318/328 Computers

Port		R/W	Description	Destination
Hex	Dec			
10	16	W	Write data port	Printer
11	17	W	Data strobe	Printer
12	18	R	Status (Bit 0 = 0 for READY)	Printer
20	32	R	Receiver Buffer Register	Modem
		W	Divisor Latch (Least significant)	Modem
		W	Transmitter Holding Buffer Register	Modem
21	33	W	Divisor Latch (Most significant)	Modem
		W	Interrupt Enable Register	Modem
22	34	W	Interrupt Identification Register	Modem
23	35	W	Line Control Register	Modem
24	36	W	Write Modem Control Register	Modem
25	37	R	Line Status Register	Modem
26	38	R	Read Modem Status Register	Modem
28	40	R	Receiver Buffer Reg. (Least Sig.)	RS-232
		W	Divisor Buffer Register	RS-232
		W	Transmitter Holding Buffer Reg.	RS-232
29	41	W	Divisor Latch (Most Sig.)	RS-232
		W	Interrupt Enable Register	RS-232
2A	42	W	Interrupt Identification Reg.	RS-232
2B	43	W	Line Control Register	RS-232
2C	44	W	Modem Control Register	RS-232
2D	45	R	Line Status Register	RS-232
2E	46	R	Modem Status Register	RS-232
30	48	R	FD-1793 Status Register	DISK
		W	FD-1793 Command Register	DISK
31	49	R/W	FD-1793 Track Register	DISK
32	50	R/W	FD-1793 Sector Register	DISK
33	51	R/W	FD-1793 Data Register	DISK
34	52	R	Read Intrq and Drq O/P Pins	DISK
		W	Disk Select Register BIT 0 = 0 Disk 1, BIT 0 = 1 Disk 2	DISK
38	56	W	Density Select Register BIT 0 = 0 Double Density BIT 0 = 1 Single Density	DISK
50	80	W	Address Register Select	80-COL- CARD

Port		R/W	Description	Destination
Hex	Dec			
51	81	W	CRT Controller Register (R0-R17)	80-COL-CARD
52	82	W	CRT Bank Control (FF = Bank On, 00 = Bank Off)	80-COL-CARD
80	128	W	TMS-9918A Write Mode=0	VDP
81	129	W	TMS-9918A Write Mode=1	VDP
84	132	R	TMS-9918A Read Mode=0	VDP
85	133	R	TMS-9918A Read Mode=1	VDP
88	136	W	AY-3-8910 Latch Address	PSG
8C	140	W	AY-3-8910 Write	PSG
90	144	R	AY-3-8910 Read	PSG
96	150	W	Write 8255 Port C	PPI
97	151	W	Write 8255 Control Word Reg.	PPI
98	152	R	Read 8255 Port A	PPI
99	153	R	Read 8255 Port B	PPI

MSX Computers

Port		R/W	Description	Destination
Hex	Dec			
80	128			RS232C
90	144	R	Busy State – bit 1	PRINTER
90	144	W	Strobe Output – bit 0	PRINTER
91	145	W	Print Data	PRINTER
98	152	R/W	Video RAM Data	VDP
99	153	R/W	Command and Status Register	VDP
A0	160	W	Address Latch	PSG
A1	161	W	Data Write	PSG
A2	162	R	Data Read	PSG
A8	168	R/W	Port A	PPI
A9	169	R/W	Port B	PPI
AA	170	R/W	Port C	PPI
AB	171	R/W	Mode Register	PPI
B0-B3	176-179	R/W	Sony Hit-Bit	External Memory
B4	180	R/W	Spectravideo X'Press	Calendar Clock
B8-BB	184	R/W	Sanyo	Light Pen
D0-D7	208-216	R/W		DISK
F7	247s	W	Bit 4 – AV Control (L-TV)	Audio/Video
		W	Bit 5 – Ym Control (L-TV)	Audio/Video
		W	Bit 6 – Ys Control (Super-TV)	Audio/Video
		W	Bit 7 – Video Select (L-TV)	Audio/Video

Index

www.ingramcontent.com/pod-product-compliance
Lightning Source LLC
Chambersburg PA
CBHW020910180526
45163CB00007B/2700

* 9 7 8 1 5 2 0 7 1 8 2 3 1 *